ABOUT THE AUTHOR

Brian M. Stratton is a Department of Transport Approved Driving
He also holds the following qualifications:

RoSPA Diploma
Cardington 'Special' Driving Test Grade A
DIAmond Advanced Instructor
The Diploma in Driving Instruction
RAC Registered Instructor
Member of IAM, DIA, MSA, GEM

He has attended and successfully completed a Police Better Driving Course
(including skid-pan training) and several Rally Driving courses.

Having successfully taught many learner drivers to pass first time,
and by 'sitting in' on many driving tests, he has gained considerable knowledge of
both the test itself and the examiner's requirements.

Two other driving reference books by the same author are:
HILL START BLUES: A New Driving Manual For The 1990s and ADI PART III: Essential Information.

About the Illustrator

Ali Clarke works as a freelance graphic designer specialising in humorous illustrations. After graduating with a B.A. Honours degree from U.C.W. Aberystwyth in '84, she moved into the world of design and print. A keen gardener and 'green', Ali now lives near Henley with an assortment of free range vegetables.

About the 'Green' Contributor

Annette Dudek B.Ed., Cert.Ed., has been actively involved with 'Friends of the Earth' since January 1990 and is concerned about all environmental issues. Despite juggling a hectic family life with a part-time teaching job, she manages to find time to write articles about green topics.

ALSO BY THE SAME AUTHOR

HILL START BLUES
A New Driving Manual for the 1990s

- All driving tasks are explained in a clear and logical manner with diagrams where necessary.
- The new syllabus for learner drivers (as recommended by the D.S.A. (Driving Standards Agency) is fully explained, along with proposed changes to the driving test.
- The unique layout of the this book presents vital information in a very user-friendly style.

Size A5 paperback

ISBN: 0-9514415-6-6

ADI PART III
Essential Information

- A completely new manual for candidates taking the Part III of the A.D.I. exam.
- All recent changes are fully explained and detailed chapters give suggested wordings for every topic.
- Clear and concise, this book is a must for anyone involved in Part III training, and will be an invaluable addition to any training course.
- Laser printed for high quality reproduction.

Size A4 Presentation in binder

ISBN: 0-9514415-4-X

For further details on these titles please contact the publishers
First Time (Driving)
Telephone: (0860) 260720

THE DRIVING TEST
Graphic Traffic Version

by

Brian M Stratton

Published by **First Time (Driving)**

Telephone: (0860) 260720

© Copyright Brian M Stratton 1991

Made and printed in Great Britain by
The Guernsey Press Co. Ltd, Guernsey, Channel Islands.

First Published
September 1991
Reprinted October 1991

© Brian M Stratton

ISBN: 0-9514415-7-4

Design and Text: Brian M Stratton

Illustration: Alison F Clarke (0734) 404931.

'Green' Driver's Guide: Annette C Dudek

Typesetting: Uppercase (0734) 475810.

The road signs are reproduced with the permission of the controller of Her Majesty's Stationery Office.

The driving test statistics are reproduced courtesy of the Directorate of Statistics at the Department of Transport.

INTRODUCTION

- The driving test presents a situation unlike any other you are likely to come across. On test your every move as a candidate will be closely watched by an examiner. Because of this many legends and misconceptions have evolved about the driving test.

- This book has been designed to explain clearly and comprehensively exactly what the test consists of, what will happen, and how to prepare yourself for it.

- This book will complement the driving lessons you have from an ADI (Approved Driving Instructor) and will help you to present yourself at the Test Centre in a confident and knowledgeable frame of mind.

- Information for this book has been gathered from various sources:

  * Accompanying candidates on test

  * Discussing the subject with driving test examiners

  * Listening to candidates' queries regarding the driving test

- Having taken all of the above into account, this book presents accurate information in a clear, easy-to-read style which is enhanced by humorous illustrations.

CONTENTS

CHAPTER 1

WHY DO WE HAVE A DRIVING TEST?

* The driving test was introduced with one aim: to reduce the number of road accidents.

* With the growing number of vehicles on the road, deaths caused by road accidents increased alarmingly.

* The Ministry of Transport decided that a 'test of competence to drive' was needed.

So . . . let's go back in time and see how it all started . . .

. . . not that far back!

Before 1st April 1934, all you had to do to get a licence was pay your money . . .

. . . even if you had never driven a car before . . .

Needless to say, this resulted in many accidents.

* In August 1934 a draft of the test regulations was circulated amongst various motoring organisations.

* Regulations were made on 4th March 1935. Applicants for driving tests were able to submit themselves voluntarily by mid-March.

So, Mr L. Hore-Belisha (the Minister of Transport) set the wheels in motion to bring in a compulsory 'test of competence to drive'.

Why Do We Have A Driving Test?

1935: PREPARING FOR THE TEST

ACCOMPANYING PERSON HAD TO BE A CURRENT DRIVERS LICENCE HOLDER WHO HAD PASSED THE TEST, OR SOMEONE WHO HAD HELD A LICENCE FOR NOT LESS THAN 2 YEARS

A 'learners' licence could be obtained for 5 shillings (25p). This was valid for 3 months.

1ST JUNE 1935: TAKING THE TEST

EXAMINERS MET CANDIDATES AT PRE-ARRANGED SITES — NO TEST CENTRES THEN!

PARP

Initially the driving test cost 7/6d (37½p). Having passed, a licence for a year cost 5 shillings.

THE WAR YEARS 1939 – '45

IN 1941 THE POPULATION WAS 46.9 MILLION. THERE WERE 2.5 MILLION VEHICLES ON THE ROADS, 9,169 PEOPLE WERE KILLED BY THEM. THIS STAGGERINGLY HIGH FIGURE WAS LARGELY DUE TO PEDESTRIANS AND CYCLISTS BEING RUN-DOWN IN THE BLACK OUT (WARTIME LIGHTING RESTRICTIONS).

WOT NO TESTS?

Driving tests were suspended. Petrol was rationed. Only essential journeys were made. At night, vehicles drove on masked lights.

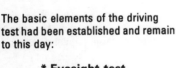

The basic elements of the driving test had been established and remain to this day:

* Eyesight test
* 'Natural' drive
* Special exercises
* Busier roads

Driving tests resumed in 1946, petrol supply was still restricted, allowing 180 miles per month. The country was still affected by the aftermath of war.

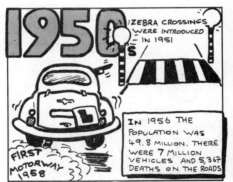

1950's

ZEBRA CROSSINGS WERE INTRODUCED IN 1951

IN 1956 THE POPULATION WAS 49.8 MILLION. THERE WERE 7 MILLION VEHICLES AND 5,367 DEATHS ON THE ROADS

FIRST MOTORWAY 1958

As petrol rationing ended, the ownership of vehicles increased considerably. A new era of hope, opportunism (and Formica!) was ahead . . .

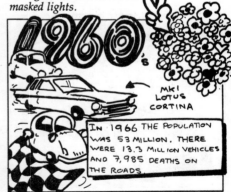

1960's

MKI LOTUS CORTINA

IN 1966 THE POPULATION WAS 53 MILLION. THERE WERE 13.3 MILLION VEHICLES AND 7,985 DEATHS ON THE ROADS.

The swinging sixties. A generation emerged without the shadow of war. Cars became fashion accessories – especially sports versions of standard cars.

Until 1975 arm signals were still a compulsory part of the test . . .

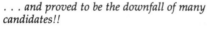

. . . and proved to be the downfall of many candidates!!

The M25 was completed in 1986; it's called the Magic Roundabout . . .

Changes in 1990 were:
* verbal debriefing at end of test for unsuccessful candidates
* Saturday tests and earlier tests, on a trial basis
* candidates must show proof of identity
* parallel parking manoeuvre introduced April 1st 1991

The test now costs £21.50, lessons range from £7 to £17.

Verbal debriefing gives candidates a much clearer idea of why they failed.

Saturday tests were tried as a way of reducing long waiting times at certain test centres.

Why Do We Have A Driving Test?

CHANGES FOR THE BETTER 3

MR WINKIE, WOULD YOU SIGN AGAINST YOUR NAME PLEASE

8 AM – IS THIS FOR **REAL** OR WHAT?

Starting tests earlier at 8 am and 8.30 am proved unsuccessful. Candidates got stuck in the morning rush hour – tests took up to 50 minutes!

CHANGES FOR THE BETTER 4

MR JONES WOULD YOU SIGN AGAINST YOUR NAME PLEASE

MAY I SEE YOUR DRIVING LICENCE

PASSPORT

DRIVING LICENCE

WORK I.D. CARD

Candidates for test must show proof of identity: a signed driving licence or other valid proof; passport etc. Only one form of ID is required.

...5 REVERSE PARKING

THIS EXERCISE DEMONSTRATES A CANDIDATES ABILITY TO:

* CO-ORDINATE THE CONTROLS
* OBSERVE WITH DUE REGARD FOR ALL OTHER ROAD USERS
* BE REASONABLY ACCURATE IN POSITIONING

THE EXAMINER WILL CHOOSE TWO OUT OF THREE EXERCISES: REVERSE PARKING TURNING-IN-THE-ROAD, REVERSE AROUND A CORNER.

Reverse parking behind a single parked car. Candidates may be asked to carry out this exercise on test.

EEC HARMONISATION

* The UK driving test will be similar to other E.E.C. member countries.
* The breakdown of trade barriers in 1992 will mean easier travel throughout Europe.
* Motorists from the continent could easily adapt to driving here and vice versa.

The Channel Tunnel opening in 1993 will facilitate motor travel throughout Europe . . .

1992 AND ALL THAT!

IT'S 1994 SOMEWHERE IN BIRMINGHAM

NEVILLE

HEY, KEVIN, DO YOU FANCY GOING TO PARIS, WE COULD DRIVE THERE IN 5 HOURS!

MEANWHILE – SOMEWHERE IN PARIS

KEVIN

GREAT IDEA NEV, WE CAN VISIT THE EIFFEL TOWER, LOUVRE, MONT MARTRE ETC...

IT WILL BE TRAY-BON.

PIERRE

VOULEZ VOUS DRIVEZ AVEC MOI TO BIRMINGHAM?

YVES

MAIS POURQUOI?

UMM..? ERR...?

Important centres will be linked . . .

SUMMARY 1
Why Do We Have A Driving Test?

* Due to increased traffic the test has become more demanding
* Remember that, although cars and roads are safer now, 95% of all accidents are caused by human error – the nut holding the steering wheel!
* Driving tests ensure that drivers have reached a certain basic standard of competence

CHAPTER 2

CHOOSING AN INSTRUCTOR

* Learning to drive is something you only do once.

* It is worth investing in a skill which will be for life.

* Getting the best tuition you can will be worth it. Your life may even be saved by it.

* Don't look for the cheapest tuition – get the best you can afford.

Many people consider themselves 'good drivers' – but can they impart that skill to others?

It is not a good idea to be taught by close family or friends . . .

A professional instructor will teach you in a safe and structured way.

Any person giving driving tuition for payment must be a Department of Transport Approved Driving Instructor. . .

. . . and display a valid certificate of registration (or licence) in the window when tuition is given.

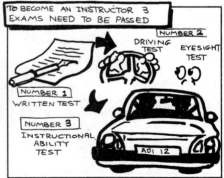

To be entered on the register of Approved Driving Instructors a person has to pass 3 separate exams . . .

Choosing An Instructor

The first step to becoming an instructor is to fulfil the criteria of the Department of Transport:

* Held a full unrestricted British Licence for at least 4 years.

* Not been disqualified in the previous 4 years.

* Be a fit and proper person.

Would-be instructors must have a very high standard of knowledge of all aspects of driving.

The first exam (part 1) is a written test of 100 multiple choice questions.

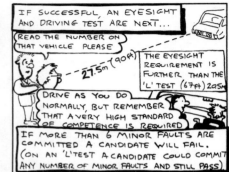

The part 2 of the exam is a test of eye sight and driving technique. Only 3 attempts are allowed. The test lasts 1 hour.

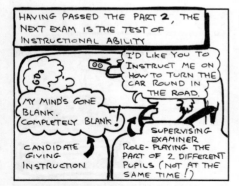

The part 3 is a test of instructional ability to ensure that effective teaching is taking place. Only 3 attempts are allowed.

Having qualified, an instructor's work is checked on a regular basis to ensure that high standards are maintained.

Only A.D.I.s have the necessary training and skills to teach effectively and safely . . .

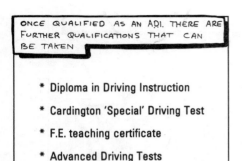

Any of the above qualifications suggest that an instructor is interested in furthering his or her career.

Think carefully before choosing an instructor. Ask around your family and friends to see if they can recommend an instructor.

Remember that the cheapest is not always the best. "You pay peanuts, you get monkeys" has been said before!

If you want a non-smoking woman instructor who doesn't have other pupils in the car then say so!

Always try to be punctual for lessons. Instructors work to set times. Think about your lesson beforehand.

Reading about a subject before a lesson will give you a grounding in the theory, and make it easier for you to understand.

7

Choosing An Instructor

Ask your instructor's advice about practising with family and friends.

Remember that the law has changed regarding accompanying drivers.

Check that you will be properly insured to drive when you practice.

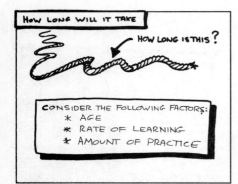

There is much more to driving than passing a test. Learn at your own pace, and don't rush things.

Developing the right attitude is vital to safe driving. This will come with good tuition and experience.

SUMMARY 2
Choosing An Instructor

* Ideally, ask around for recommendations
* Ask Instructors about qualifications and teaching methods
* Follow any advice you are given
* Be realistic – learning a life-skill won't happen overnight

CHAPTER 3 — APPLYING FOR A DRIVING TEST

* Take your Driving Instructor's advice as to when you'll be ready to take your test.

* You apply for a Driving Test appointment on a form DL26.

* You can get this form from most Post Offices, or your Instructor will supply you with one.

Your Driving Instructor will be the best person to tell you when you are ready to take the test . . .

Read the notes carefully before filling in the form.

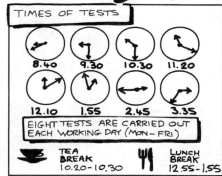

Ask your Instructor about any part you're not sure about . . .

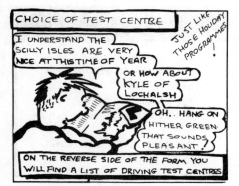

Generally, your Instructor will advise you to choose a local test centre.

Waiting times for tests vary from centre to centre – the average waiting time is approximately 10 weeks.

Be as flexible as you can regarding dates and times. Restricting yourself can only increase the time you have to wait.

Applying For A Driving Test

If you cannot speak English or are deaf, you may have an interpreter sitting in on the test.

If you're unsure about this, ask your Instructor's advice.

Your Driving Instructor will inform you of the current fee. It is also displayed in test centres.

Send the form and fee to the DSA office for the area where you want to be tested.

You can make only one application at a time.

SUMMARY 3
Applying For A Driving Test

* Your instructor will be the best person to tell you when to apply
* Use form DL26
* Read the notes carefully
* Send the correct fee to the correct address
* Having sent off the form, expect notification within 2 weeks

* A white card (DL28) will be sent to you advising you of the date, time and place.

* If you haven't received a card within 21 days, contact the Traffic Area Office.

* When you have received your card, keep it safe!

Expect a white post-card, notifying you of your test date.

Take the card along to your next driving lesson . . .

And then keep it safe – perhaps with your driving licence.

There must be 10 clear working days notice given if you need to postpone or cancel the test without forfeiting the fee.

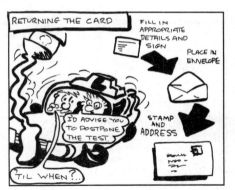

If your Instructor has advised you to postpone your test accept his advice – it will be in your best interests!

You should get a new appointment card within 2 weeks.

Notification Of Test Appointment

The number of Tests taken has risen over the past 10 years.

Latest figures available show that slightly more women take the test.

Predictably the under 21's predominate in the test.

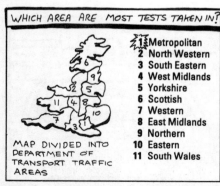

The Metropolitan area (London and environs) contains a greater population than any other area, hence it's Number 1 position.

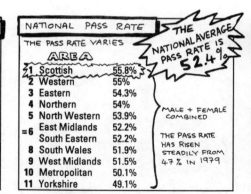

Highest pass rate = 61.7% (Scottish male)
Lowest pass rate = 44.6% (Yorkshire female)

SUMMARY 4
Notification Of Test Appointment

* As soon as you receive your appointment card, check the details.

* Inform your Instructor of the date, time and place

* If you need to change the date, 10 clear working days' notice must be given, otherwise the fee is forfeit

Most people have pre-conceived ideas about driving examiners . . .

'Experts' put forward theories on the examiners.

And over the years many stories have evolved about them . . .

Usually started by people who have failed the Test . . .

And who try to think up reasons why they failed.

However, the examiners are not like that at all . . .

Spotlight On The Examiners

THE TRUTH ABOUT EXAMINERS....

COMMERCE

DRIVING INSTRUCTORS

INDUSTRY

TEACHERS

EXAMINERS COME FROM ALL WALKS OF LIFE

Although some examiners have been driving instructors this is not a necessary requirement.

APPLYING FOR THE JOB...

* Certain criteria must be fulfilled to apply for the Job of Examiner.
* Aged at least 25.
* Good health and eyesight.
* Ability to get on with people.
* Interest in motoring and road safety.
* High standard of driving.
* No motoring or other convictions.
  (Open to male and female applicants)

Having satisfied the above criteria, the next step is to take a special driving test . . .

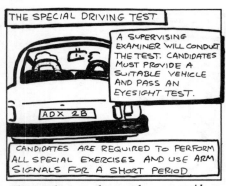

THE SPECIAL DRIVING TEST

A SUPERVISING EXAMINER WILL CONDUCT THE TEST. CANDIDATES MUST PROVIDE A SUITABLE VEHICLE AND PASS AN EYESIGHT TEST.

ADX 2B

CANDIDATES ARE REQUIRED TO PERFORM ALL SPECIAL EXERCISES AND USE ARM SIGNALS FOR A SHORT PERIOD.

This test lasts one hour and covers a wide variety of roads: urban, rural, motorway etc. A very high standard is required.

A VERY GOOD KNOWLEDGE OF THE HIGHWAY CODE AND OTHER MOTORING MATTERS IS REQUIRED

AND WHAT'S THE RULE REGARDING THE USE OF HAZARD WARNING LIGHTS?

TO WARN OTHERS OF A TEMPORARY OBSTRUCTION

CANDIDATES WILL BE ASKED TO IDENTIFY SOME TRAFFIC SIGNS, AND ALSO TO ANSWER SOME QUESTIONS ON THE HIGHWAY CODE AND OTHER MOTORING MATTERS

At the end of the driving part, candidates will be asked questions on the Highway Code.

THE SUPERVISING EXAMINER WILL ALSO DISCUSS MATTERS OF GENERAL INTEREST RELATING TO THE MOTORING SCENE.

...AND WHAT DO YOU THINK ABOUT THESE TRAFFIC CALMING SCHEMES?

YES, I THINK GENERALLY THEY'RE A GOOD IDEA

Candidates are expected to show an interest in all aspects of motoring.

GETTING THE RESULT....

AFTER THE SPECIAL DRIVING TEST, THE SUPERVISING EXAMINER SUBMITS A REPORT

TO THE RECRUITMENT SECTION AT THE D.S.A.

Looks LIKE THE LETTER'S ARRIVED!

WHO THEN WRITE TO THE CANDIDATE

Candidates are not told the result of the test immediately . . . they have to wait . . .

If successful on the special driving test, candidates will be invited for an interview.

If considered suitable, a candidate would then be sent on a four week residential training course at the Driving Establishment.

At Cardington in Bedfordshire, 2 weeks of the course is spent on further improving the candidate's own driving.

Teaching and examining would cause a conflict of interest . . .

*therefore examiners exclusively **Test** candidates, whilst instructors exclusively **Teach** pupils.*

A new examiner is 'on probation' for the first 12 months.

During this 'probationary' period an examiner's work is closely monitored.

You could walk past an examiner in the street and not recognise one . . .

If you listened to their conversation you would find it very everyday . . .

The career structure for a driving examiner is clearly defined, promotion is always from within.

Women now make up about 5% of the total examiner workforce.

SUMMARY 5
Spotlight On The Examiners

* Examiners come from all walks of life
* Many have been Instructors, but it is not a necessity
* Rigorous training ensures a uniformity of standards
* Examiners' work is continually monitored and assessed

You will need to demonstrate that you can:

* Handle your vehicle safely.

* Show courtesy and consideration to other road users.

* Observe the Highway Code.

Examiners do not look for perfection, but a basic standard of safe driving.

EXAMINERS WILL TEST YOU ON...

THE EYESIGHT TEST

WILL YOU READ THE NUMBER ON THE VEHICLE OVER THERE.

I SEE NO SHIPS!

IF YOU CANNOT READ A NUMBER PLATE AT THE SPECIFIED DISTANCE THE TEST WILL NOT PROCEED

To make sure you are safe, examiners consider all aspects of your drive.

KNOWING IT AND SHOWING IT

KNOW THE HIGHWAY CODE

IN THEORY

YEAH, I KNOW THIS ONE — WARNING OF TED ROGERS

*AND IN PRACTICE

At the end of the test you will be asked questions on the Highway Code and other motoring matters.

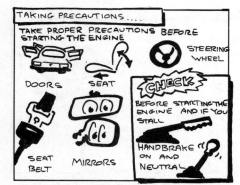

TAKING PRECAUTIONS....

TAKE PROPER PRECAUTIONS BEFORE STARTING THE ENGINE

STEERING WHEEL

DOORS   SEAT

CHECK BEFORE STARTING THE ENGINE AND IF YOU STALL

HANDBRAKE ON AND NEUTRAL

SEAT BELT   MIRRORS

Always carry out the safety checks in the logical order you have been taught.

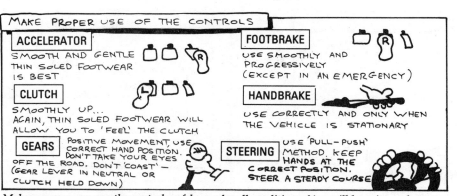

MAKE PROPER USE OF THE CONTROLS

ACCELERATOR
SMOOTH AND GENTLE THIN SOLED FOOTWEAR IS BEST

CLUTCH
SMOOTHLY UP... AGAIN, THIN SOLED FOOTWEAR WILL ALLOW YOU TO 'FEEL' THE CLUTCH

GEARS POSITIVE MOVEMENT, USE CORRECT HAND POSITION. DON'T TAKE YOUR EYES OFF THE ROAD. DON'T 'COAST' — (GEAR LEVER IN NEUTRAL OR CLUTCH HELD DOWN)

FOOTBRAKE
USE SMOOTHLY AND PROGRESSIVELY (EXCEPT IN AN EMERGENCY)

HANDBRAKE
USE CORRECTLY AND ONLY WHEN THE VEHICLE IS STATIONARY

STEERING USE 'PULL-PUSH' METHOD. KEEP HANDS AT THE CORRECT POSITION. STEER A STEADY COURSE

Make sure you can use the controls safely, under all conditions. You will be using at least two of these controls simultaneously, so be competent and confident.

Look properly when you check, and act sensibly on what you see.

Co-ordinate the controls and move away smoothly and safely.

A quick reaction is necessary here. Avoid locking the wheels or skidding.

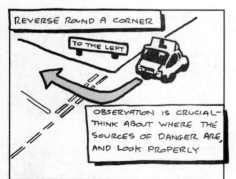

If you were to take the test in a van you would be asked to reverse to the right.

This is not necessarily a 'three-point-turn'!

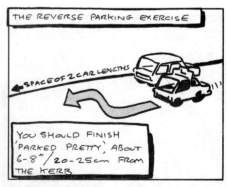

This exercise will be carried out behind a single parked vehicle.

Firstly, make sure your mirrors are clean, properly adjusted and free from obstructions.

Just looking in your mirrors isn't enough; you must act sensibly on what you see.

Use only signals as illustrated in the Highway Code.

Look well ahead and plan your driving to give yourself time to react.

Be ready to slow down or keep your speed down.

On the other hand you must not drive too slowly – this will endanger and inconvenience other road users.

What The Examiners Look For

Being over-cautious is dangerous – other road users become confused, frustrated and angry.

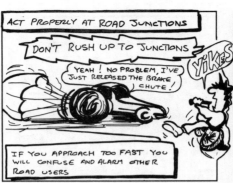

Approach junctions at the correct speed, being prepared to stop if necessary.

Look properly and act sensibly on what you see. Don't make other road users change speed or direction.

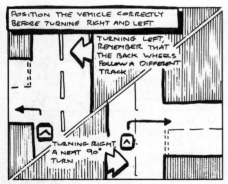

Turning at the correct point will put you in the best position to enter the new road.

Ensure that you can see clearly into the road before turning.

Before overtaking, ask yourself "is it necessary"? It very rarely is.

20

Read the road well ahead and plan your drive. Always be prepared to . . .

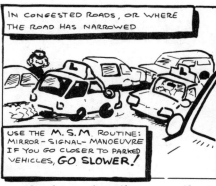

. . . slow down and stop if necessary. Always put yourself in a safe position.

This situation calls for very careful judgement of speed and distance.

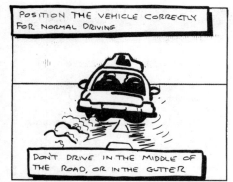

Your normal driving position should be 3ft/1m from the kerb or parked vehicles . . .

If you cannot allow that much clearance GO SLOWER!

Treat Zebra crossings as an extension of the pavement – pedestrians have precedence!

What The Examiners Look For

Make sure you pull up somewhere safe and convenient. The Highway Code and common sense should guide you.

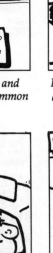

Read the road well ahead – anticipate and give yourself time to react.

To avoid conflict, an examiner will alert a candidate to danger. Obviously, this would cause you to fail the test.

This would cause you to fail the test, for obvious reasons.

The driving test is designed to ensure that a minimum safe standard (at least!) is attained by those who pass.

SUMMARY 6
What The Examiners Look For

* Safe handling of the vehicle

* Safe operation of controls under varying conditions

* Consideration and courtesy towards all other road users

* Complying with the Highway Code

* All tests are carried out in a uniform manner.
* Examiners will use set phrases and directions.
* Your Driving Instructor should use the same terms to direct you.
* This will enable you to familiarise yourself with the terminology.

Despite rumours to the contrary, examiners do not speak a different language.

Directions are given clearly and unambiguously

Take the next road on the left please

Yeah, that's clear

All examiners are trained to give directions in the same way.

Before you drive away

I'd like you to follow the road ahead unless the traffic signs direct you otherwise, or unless I ask you to turn which I'll do in good time.

Move off when you're ready please

START

JELLY IMPRESSION

At crossroads and traffic lights, follow the road ahead (when safe!).

When the examiner wants you to pull up...

I'd like you to pull up on the left, please

Must check mirror first, then signal if necessary

Ensure you choose somewhere safe and convenient.

And when he wants you to drive on...

Drive on when you're ready please

Watch out for sources of danger hidden in blind spots

HP

Heinz 57

Before you move away, make sure it's safe to do so.

Before the emergency stop the examiner will ask you to pull up on the left and will say...

Very shortly I shall ask you to stop as in an emergency, the signal will be like this, STOP!

When I do that I want you to stop immediately and under full control, as though a child had run off the pavement. Drive on when you're ready please

Yeah no problem mate... watch this

It is not necessary to respond verbally to instructions.

How The Examiners Phrase Directions

The examiner's wording here prevents any further uncalled for emergency stops.

You will have carried out these exercises with your Instructor and will be familiar with the wording . . .

However, let the examiner finish giving you the instructions first!

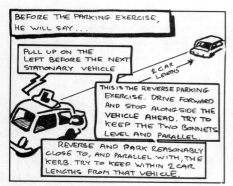

This exercise will always be carried out behind one parked vehicle.

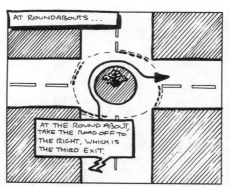

This is just one example. Obviously the road layout will dictate the examiner's precise phrasing.

Directions will be given in good time, allowing you to react safely and correctly.

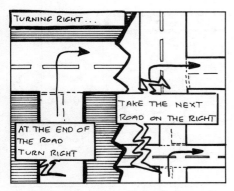

Don't get your right and left mixed up — it could be dangerous!

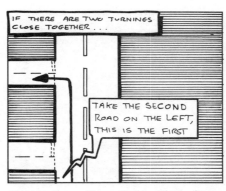

The examiner will usually identify the first road as you approach.

The examiner will adapt his phrasing to make it absolutely clear as to where he wants you to go.

Listen carefully to the directions — they will be precisely phrased.

Don't try to engage the examiner in conversation: concentrate on your driving!

Use your initiative and demonstrate to the examiner that you can handle any situation safely.

How The Examiners Phrase Directions

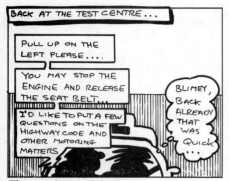

The examiner will direct you to a suitable parking place.

There will be approximately 6 questions and 6 signs to identify.

Keep calm, listen to what the examiner says and show him your driving licence.

Accept the examiner's decision with good grace. Do not argue with him!

. . . He will tell you what error(s) led you to fail.

SUMMARY 7
How The Examiners Phrase Directions

* All wording is concise and clear
* Terms used avoid confusion or misunderstanding
* Phrases used are standard throughout the UK
* Safety is always the paramount consideration

* The driving test is straightforward.

* Candidates fail if they commit driving faults which could, or actually do, cause danger or inconvenience to other road users.

* If you commit only minor faults you will pass.

The marking system of the test is clearly defined.

MARKING THE FORM

THE EXAMINER WILL HAVE THIS WITH HIM IN THE CAR

Marks are put down on a standard form: DL.25 (Driving Test Report).

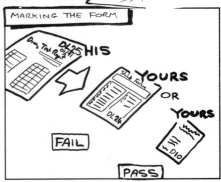

MARKING THE FORM

HIS

YOURS

OR

YOURS

FAIL

PASS

The report form is for the use of the examiner . . .

OTHER DETAILS

Also on the form will be details of the car, make and registration number, and time of the test.

DURING THE TEST

DON'T TRY AND SEE WHAT THE EXAMINER IS WRITING — CONCENTRATE ON YOUR DRIVING

The examiner will have his report form on his lap during the test . . .

DON'T PANIC

OH NO! I SAW HIM WRITING SOMETHING DOWN... THAT'S IT I'VE FAILED, I KNOW I HAVE...

AAAAGHH!

I WISH HE'D SETTLE DOWN...

If you see the examiner mark something down on his form, don't worry . . .

How The Test Is Marked

It was probably a minor fault; don't dwell on it, just concentrate on what is happening.

If a candidate fails it means the examiner has more paperwork to do than if the candidate passes!

The examiner will also note down details such as weather conditions . . .

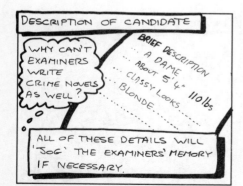

A brief description of the candidate (needed for possible recollection at a later date).

And also remarks; this is for details of any faults which led to failure, or anything of note that happened.

Also noted will be the number of the Pass Certificate (D10) or Statement of Failure (DL24).

The marks on the form will then be transferred to the Statement of Failure (DL24), or you will get a Pass Certificate (D10).

On returning to the test centre after each test, examiners complete the relevant paperwork.

At the end of each working day, completed paperwork is sent off to DSA headquarters.

Examiners assess the cause of an error, not the effect.

This is then marked as appropriate on the form.

If you have unsuccessfully taken a test you will have been given a Statement of Failure.

How The Test Is Marked

Minor faults are marked with a short diagonal stroke, right to left.

Serious faults are marked with an X.

Dangerous faults are marked with a capital 'D'.

In this example, the driver has cut a corner when the view is clear.

Here, the driver has cut the corner but couldn't see – fortunately no other road users were about. This is potentially dangerous.

In this example the driver has cut the corner, causing another road user to brake and swerve. This is actually dangerous.

IF YOU'VE FAILED...

DRIVING
STANDARDS
AGENCY

STATEMENT OF FAILURE
ROAD TRAFFIC ACT 1988

NAME
TEST CENTRE
DATE
AUTHORISED BY EXAMINER

1 ☒
2 ☐
3 ☐
4 ☐
5 ☐
6 ☐
7 ☐
8 ☐
9 ☐
10 ☐
11 ☐

12 ☐
13 ☐
14 ☐
15 ☐
16 ☐
17 ☐
18 ☐
19 ☐
20 ☐
21 ☒

DL 24 (01/91)

THE ITEM(S) THAT CAUSED YOU TO FAIL WILL BE MARKED.

If you have a Statement of Failure (there are 21 items marked on the sheet), the following information may be helpful.

1 EYESIGHT

IF YOU CAN'T READ THE NUMBER PLATE, AFTER TWO ATTEMPTS THE EXAMINER WILL GET A TAPE TO MEASURE THE EXACT DISTANCE

If your eyesight isn't up to standard it would be dangerous for you to drive!!

2 KNOWING THE HIGHWAY CODE

REASON FOR FAILING

LACK OF KNOWLEDGE OF THE HIGHWAY CODE; COMPREHENSION INADEQUATE.

You can fail on the Highway Code alone if your answers are dangerous.

3 TAKE PROPER PRECAUTIONS BEFORE STARTING THE ENGINE

REASON FOR FAILING

NOT CHECKING THAT THE HANDBRAKE IS ON, AND GEAR LEVER IS IN NEUTRAL BEFORE STARTING OR RE-STARTING THE ENGINE.
ADJUSTING MIRRORS ETC. WHILST ON THE MOVE.

This is obviously dangerous if other users are affected by your actions.

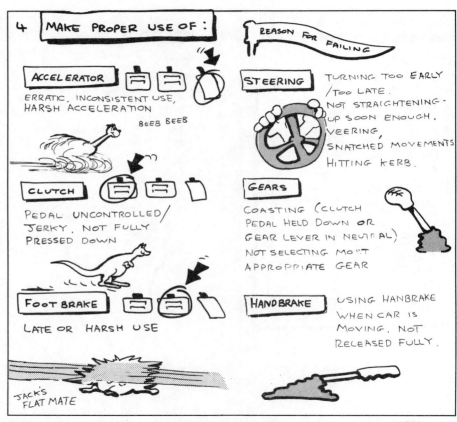

4 MAKE PROPER USE OF:

REASON FOR FAILING

ACCELERATOR
ERRATIC, INCONSISTENT USE, HARSH ACCELERATION

BEEB BEEB

CLUTCH
PEDAL UNCONTROLLED/ JERKY. NOT FULLY PRESSED DOWN

FOOT BRAKE
LATE OR HARSH USE

JACK'S FLAT MATE

STEERING
TURNING TOO EARLY /TOO LATE.
NOT STRAIGHTENING- UP SOON ENOUGH.
VEERING, SNATCHED MOVEMENTS
HITTING KERB.

GEARS
COASTING (CLUTCH PEDAL HELD DOWN OR GEAR LEVER IN NEUTRAL)
NOT SELECTING MOST APPROPRIATE GEAR

HANDBRAKE
USING HANBRAKE WHEN CAR IS MOVING. NOT RELEASED FULLY.

*Mis-use of any of these controls could be dangerous. Remember that as a driver, **YOU** are responsible for your car's position, speed and conduct on the road.*

5 MOVE AWAY SAFELY / UNDER CONTROL

REASON FOR FAILING

NOT LOOKING PROPERLY BEFORE MOVING AWAY

WATCH IT MATE!

REASON FOR FAILING

UNDER CONTROL:

STALLING
NOT COORDINATING CONTROLS
MOVING AWAY TOO FAST

OOPS!

SCREECHING TYRES

When you move away it is dangerous to cause others to change speed or direction.

6 STOP VEHICLE IN AN EMERGENCY

REASON FOR FAILING

PROMPTLY:
SLOW REACTION, INADEQUATE BRAKING

UNDER CONTROL:
SKIDDING (UNCORRECTED)
WRONG PEDAL USED.
TAKING HAND(S) OFF THE WHEEL
USING HANDBRAKE

I CAN'T BEAR TO LOOK

It is dangerous to skid or lock the wheels; you will have no steering control.

7 REVERSE INTO A LIMITED OPENING TO THE RIGHT OR LEFT

REASON FOR FAILING

UNDER CONTROL:
HITTING THE KERB.
GOING TOO WIDE
GOING TOO FAST / UNCONTROLLED
STALLING

WITH DUE REGARD FOR OTHER ROAD USERS:
NOT KEEPING A PROPER LOOKOUT.
NOT ACTING ON WHAT WAS SEEN.
NOT USING MIRROR(S) WHEN STOPPING OR STARTING MANOEUVRE.

Think about the dangers involved in this manoeuvre, and how you could affect all other road users.

8 TURN ROUND BY MEANS OF FORWARD AND REVERSE GEARS

REASON FOR FAILING

UNDER CONTROL:

NOT CO-ORDINATING THE GAS / CLUTCH / STEERING. TAKING MORE TURNS THAN NECESSARY. STALLING, HITTING THE KERB.

WITH DUE REGARD FOR OTHER ROAD USERS:

NOT BEING READY TO STOP AND LET TRAFFIC PASS. NOT LOOKING PROPERLY. NOT KEEPING A PROPER LOOKOUT.

9 REVERSE PARK

REASON FOR FAILING

UNDER CONTROL:

INADEQUATE CONTROL CAUSING EXCESSIVE 'SHUNTING'. STOPPING TOO WIDE / NOT PARALLEL, STALLING.

TOUCHING THE KERB. MORE THAN TWO VEHICLE LENGTHS AWAY.

WITH DUE REGARD FOR OTHER ROAD USERS:

USING MIRRORS ONLY. POOR OBSERVATION. NOT ACTING ON WHAT WAS SEEN

10 MAKE EFFECTIVE USE OF MIRROR(S) WELL BEFORE:

REASON FOR FAILING

SIGNALLING:

NOT ACTING ON WHAT WAS SEEN ACTIONS TOO LATE

CHANGING DIRECTION:

TOO LATE TO BE OF USE

SLOWING DOWN OR STOPPING:

NOT ACTING ON WHAT WAS SEEN

USING MIRRORS TOO LATE

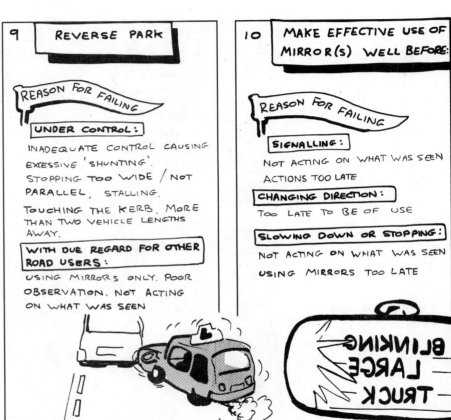

This exercise should be done in as few moves as possible. If not, you are endangering and inconveniencing other road users.

You will cause danger or inconvenience to other road users if you do not look properly or control your car properly.

It is not enough just to look at your mirrors — you must act sensibly on what you see.

11 GIVING SIGNALS

REASON FOR FAILING

WHERE NECESSARY :

NOT GIVING A NECESSARY SIGNAL

CORRECTLY :

SIGNAL GIVEN INCORRECTLY / NOT CANCELLED / MISLEADING OR DANGEROUS SIGNALS (ie, AT PEDESTRIAN CROSSINGS)

IN GOOD TIME :

SIGNAL GIVEN TOO LATE, NOT RE-APPLYING A CANCELLED SIGNAL

FRANKIE SAYS NO

If signals are not given clearly or for long enough, other road users could be dangerously misled.

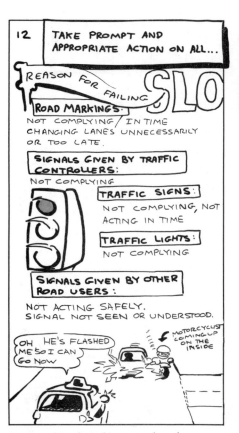

12 TAKE PROMPT AND APPROPRIATE ACTION ON ALL...

REASON FOR FAILING

SLO

ROAD MARKINGS :

NOT COMPLYING / IN TIME CHANGING LANES UNNECESSARILY OR TOO LATE.

SIGNALS GIVEN BY TRAFFIC CONTROLLERS :

NOT COMPLYING

TRAFFIC SIGNS :

NOT COMPLYING, NOT ACTING IN TIME

TRAFFIC LIGHTS :

NOT COMPLYING

SIGNALS GIVEN BY OTHER ROAD USERS :

NOT ACTING SAFELY. SIGNAL NOT SEEN OR UNDERSTOOD.

OH HE'S FLASHED ME SO I CAN GO NOW

MOTORCYCLIST COMING UP ON THE INSIDE

Signs and road markings are there for a purpose:- not acting on information could be very dangerous.

13 EXERCISE PROPER CARE IN THE USE OF SPEED.

REASON FOR FAILING

DRIVING AT A SPEED UNSUITABLE FOR ROAD / TRAFFIC / WEATHER CONDITIONS

EXCEEDING THE SPEED LIMIT.

NOT KEEPING AN ADEQUATE DISTANCE BEHIND OTHER ROAD USERS.

NOT BEING READY TO SLOW DOWN (OR KEEP SPEED DOWN).

FASTER THAN A SPEEDING BULLET

Driving too fast for the prevailing conditions could be extremely dangerous. Remember you are not the only person on the road.

14 MAKE PROGRESS BY DRIVING AT A SPEED APPROPRIATE TO THE ROAD AND TRAFFIC CONDITIONS, AVOIDING UNDUE HESITANCY

REASON FOR FAILING

DRIVING TOO SLOWLY WHEN THE ROAD IS CLEAR AND CONDITIONS ALLOW

TAKING TOO LONG TO BUILD UP SPEED. REDUCTION OF SPEED TOO EARLY.

NOT BEING PREPARED TO EMERGE AT JUNCTIONS.

OVERCAUTIOUS TO A DANGEROUS EXTENT

15 ACT PROPERLY AT ROAD JUNCTIONS

REASON FOR FAILING

REGULATE SPEED CORRECTLY ON APPROACH:
NOT SLOWING DOWN SUFFICIENTLY

TAKING EFFECTIVE OBSERVATION BEFORE EMERGING:
CAUSING OTHERS TO CHANGE SPEED/ DIRECTION. NOT LOOKING PROPERLY. STOPPING BEYOND OR KERB LINE

POSITION VEHICLE CORRECTLY BEFORE TURNING RIGHT OR LEFT:
INCORRECT POSITION
SOURCE OF DANGER LURKING

AVOID CUTTING RIGHT HAND CORNERS
CUTTING CORNERS ON RIGHT HAND TURNS

16 OVERTAKE, MEET, CROSS PATH OF OTHER VEHICLES SAFELY.

REASON FOR FAILING

OVERTAKE:
NOT OVERTAKING SAFELY

MEET:
NOT ALLOWING ADEQUATE CLEARANCE TO APPROACHING TRAFFIC. EXCESSIVE SPEED FOR SITUATION. UNCERTAIN ACTION.

CROSS:
NOT ALLOWING ADEQUATE CLEARANCE WHEN TURNING RIGHT ACROSS THE PATH OF ONCOMING TRAFFIC.

Being too slow or hesitant causes others to become confused and angry; an angry driver is a dangerous driver.

75% of all accidents happen at junctions — generally due to carelessness or lack of good judgement.

Situations which involve potential conflict (colliding with other road users) must always be dealt with safely.

17 POSITION THE VEHICLE CORRECTLY DURING NORMAL DRIVING

REASON FOR FAILING

DRIVING TOO FAR OUT FROM, OR TOO CLOSE TO, THE KERB

?!

This is obviously dangerous; you will be too close to other road users, endangering them.

18 ALLOW ADEQUATE CLEARANCE TO STATIONARY VEHICLES

REASON FOR FAILING

NOT ALLOWING ADEQUATE CLEARANCE OR TRAVELLING TOO FAST FOR THE CLEARANCE AVAILABLE.

NOT ADJUSTING SPEED WHERE SPACE IS RESTRICTED

DON'T YOU REALISE HOW CLOSE YOU'RE GOING TO THESE PARKED VEHICLES?

NO, I'M NOT SITTING ON THAT SIDE OF THE CAR.

The danger here is that going too close reduces your margin of safety if anything should happen; doors opening, pedestrians stepping out, etc.

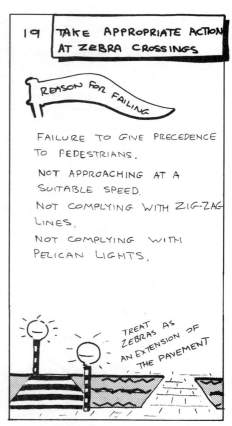

19 TAKE APPROPRIATE ACTION AT ZEBRA CROSSINGS

REASON FOR FAILING

FAILURE TO GIVE PRECEDENCE TO PEDESTRIANS.

NOT APPROACHING AT A SUITABLE SPEED.

NOT COMPLYING WITH ZIG-ZAG LINES.

NOT COMPLYING WITH PELICAN LIGHTS.

TREAT ZEBRAS AS AN EXTENSION OF THE PAVEMENT

Pedestrians have absolute precedence when on the crossings. Failure to observe this is very dangerous.

20 SELECT A SAFE POSITION FOR NORMAL STOPS

REASON FOR FAILING

NOT STOPPING PARALLEL TO, OR CLOSE TO, THE KERB.
STOPPING WHERE UNSAFE

THANK YOU, I'LL WALK TO THE KERB FROM HERE...

SWERVE

Always choose somewhere safe and convenient and park pretty!

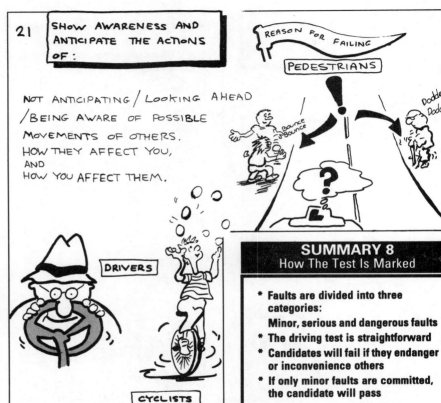

21 SHOW AWARENESS AND ANTICIPATE THE ACTIONS OF:

NOT ANTICIPATING / LOOKING AHEAD /BEING AWARE OF POSSIBLE MOVEMENTS OF OTHERS.
HOW THEY AFFECT YOU,
AND
HOW YOU AFFECT THEM.

DRIVERS

CYCLISTS

REASON FOR FAILING

PEDESTRIANS

Bounce Bounce

Dodder Dodder

?

It is your responsibility as a driver to show consideration to all other road users, especially the more vulnerable ones.

SUMMARY 8
How The Test Is Marked

* Faults are divided into three categories:
  Minor, serious and dangerous faults
* The driving test is straightforward
* Candidates will fail if they endanger or inconvenience others
* If only minor faults are committed, the candidate will pass

SHUT UP...

. . . You've been up half the night studying the Highway Code.

Wear whatever you feel most comfortable in for driving – you don't need to dress up for the examiner.

At breakfast, your sister kindly helps you out and offers words of encouragement.

Make sure you have your licence and appointment card readily to hand . . .

So, fully prepared, you should try to drive for about 1 hour before your test to re-familiarise yourself with the car.

Aim to be parked at the test centre no more than 10 minutes before your test – A final run through of the Highway Code?

The Day Of Your Test

Leave the car and walk to the waiting room at the test centre.

Take a seat and wait for the examiner to enter the waiting room.

At the time of the test your examiner will enter the waiting room and call out your name.

Go up to your examiner and sign where indicated.

He will then ask to see your driving licence (or other proof of I.D.).

You will then be asked to lead the way to your vehicle.

40

The examiner will point to a vehicle whose registration number he wants you to read.

He will then ask you to get in the car . . .

While he makes a note of the vehicle details and checks its roadworthiness.

He will then get into the front passenger seat of your vehicle, and will give you instructions.

Your instructor should have briefed you regarding this.

The first few minutes or so of the test is a 'natural drive', ie, no special exercises.

The Day Of Your Test

Your instructor will wait at the test centre (or vicinity) for your return.

Generally the first special exercise to be carried out will be the emergency stop.

Next will be one of the manoeuvres.

And then another manoeuvre !

Just because you're heading back to the test centre don't let your concentration lapse!

You could fail on the Highway Code alone, so make sure you know it!

The examiner will tell you the result after the Highway Code questions.

If you've passed the examiner will fill in and hand to you a 'Certificate of Competence to Drive'.

Your instructor will be waiting for you to return from the test.

If you fail, the examiner will hand you a 'Statement of Failure' and will tell you the fault(s) that caused you to fail.

Whether you pass or fail your instructor will drive back.

It is a good idea to get your certificate and provisional licence photo copied.

The Day Of Your Test

You may drive while you are waiting for your full licence to arrive.

You arrive home, eager to share your good news . . . a quiet reception awaits you.

And then there are all the phone calls to make . . .

And then a few more . . .

It's a great feeling when you pass your test — enjoy it!

CHAPTER 10 TALL TEST TALES

* There are probably more myths about the driving test than any other motoring subject!

* Most of these stories have been around for years

* Generally these legends will have been passed on by someone who failed the test

You will have heard many things about the test – Some fact and some fiction; your A.D.I. will tell you which is which!

During the drive examiners will not converse with candidates other than to give directions.

If you're safe enough, you'll pass first time – get enough experience and practice before taking the test.

There is not a quota system in operation; each candidate is judged on his or her own merit.

Examiners do not pre-judge candidates and the word 'fail' is never written down on any form.

If the test route takes you outside a 30mph limit, drive to as near the new limit as conditions allow.

Tall Test Tales

The day, or time, make no difference; if you're safe enough you'll pass.

Your style of dress will not impress or influence the examiner – it's your driving he's assessing, not your dress sense.

The test is straightforward. There are no tricks and directions are given clearly.

Examiners will not favour driving school cars above privately owned cars.

There are both male and female examiners ranging in age from 25 to 65; generally they are polite and courteous.

SUMMARY 10
Tall Test Tales

* Don't believe everything you hear – most of it isn't true!

* Ask your A.D.I. what is fact and what is fiction

* Most stories originate as excuses for failing!

CHAPTER 11

WHY PEOPLE FAIL ... ✗

* So leaving aside the 'reasons' described in the previous chapter ...

* Why do candidates fail tests?

* Is it the car, the Instructor, the examiner ...?

* In 99.9% of cases ... It's the driver ...

Statistics are kept for all tests, and patterns can be seen to emerge.

... THE RESULT

The fault(s) listed are either potentially or actually dangerous.

... AND THE REST OF IT.

Even though you may have only got marked down for 1 or 2 faults you probably made minor errors as well.

... RESULTS COLLECTED

Test results from all over the UK are analysed and studied.

MALE V FEMALE

These results can be broken down into male and female faults.

... MOST COMMON FAULTS

THE BIG TOP FIVE

1 IMPROPER USE OF CONTROLS
2 JUNCTION / CROSSROAD PROCEDURE
3 INEFFECTIVE USE OF MIRRORS
4 INABILITY TO REVERSE
5 FAILURE TO MAKE PROGRESS

So why is it that these contribute so much to test failure? ...

Why People Fail

Make sure you can operate the controls correctly and safely under all conditions.

Candidates fail here because of uncertainty or mis-judgement.

It is not enough just to look in your mirrors – you must act sensibly on what you see.

30% more women fail on manoeuvres than men.

Don't go especially slowly or cautiously just because it's your test – it could fail you!

SUMMARY 11
Why People Fail

* **Mainly control faults**
* **If you are aware of why such faults occur you will be able to minimise the risk of committing dangerous faults**
* **Professional tuition and practice will help to eliminate faults**

CHAPTER 12

WHAT YOU HAVE TO DO TO PASS ✓

* Drive as you do normally

* Don't put on a show for the examiner

* Demonstrate that you can handle your vehicle safely and confidently

* Remember all that you've been taught – and put it into practice

Any attempt to 'put it on' for the examiner will be seen through immediately!

CHECK AND CHECK AGAIN

REMEMBER THAT AT 30 M.P.H. TRAFFIC IS TRAVELLING AT 45 Ft/Sec

Just before moving off, don't forget to look around, and again if it's an angled start.

READ THE ROAD WELL AHEAD... PLAN YOUR DRIVE

MIRRORS, WHAT'S THAT CYCLIST DOING? MIRRORS, WHO'S THAT CAR FLASHING? MIRRORS, THAT PEDESTRIAN LOOKS UNCERTAIN...

Use all the information provided by your eyes and ears to plan your drive.

EXPERIENCE SHOWS

YES, THIS ONE IS CERTAINLY GIVING ME A GOOD DRIVE

COMPETENT CANDIDATE GETTING ON WITH IT

Through experience, examiners can usually tell how good or bad a driver is relatively quickly.

REMEMBER THE M.S.M. ROUTINE

PULL UP ON THE LEFT WHERE IT IS SAFE AND CONVENIENT PLEASE

MIRROR... INTERNAL AND DOOR SIGNAL... START SLOWING DOWN... MIRROR AGAIN

When pulling up to (or moving away from) the kerb, only signal if necessary.

THE EMERGENCY STOP

VERY SHORTLY I SHALL ASK YOU TO STOP AS IN AN EMERGENCY

MUST REMEMBER QUICK REACTION, **BBC** - BRAKE (A GOOD HARD PUSH) BEFORE CLUTCH AVOID SKIDDING. CHECK OVER BOTH SHOULDERS BEFORE MOVING AWAY.

The examiner will check behind to make sure it is safe to carry out this exercise.

What You Have To Do To Pass

During the turn-in-the-road it is generally inadvisable to wave people through. If necessary though, take control and do it.

If you're going too wide, or too close to the kerb, stop and pull forward then continue with the manoeuvre – don't ask, just do it!

On test this will always be done behind a single parked car. Practice between two, and also on the right hand side of a one way street.

Use your mirrors frequently and be alert to all road users' movements.

You will come across vehicles parked very close to junctions.

. . . Also, pedestrians or other obstacles may restrict your view.

50

At junctions where your view is restricted you will need to widen your zone of vision, so creep and peep!

Look for clues and anticipate – base your driving on what you can see, can't see and might reasonably expect to happen.

When turning right, don't commit yourself until you can see that it's safe to enter the road.

If there is insufficient room to wait in the middle, wait behind the stop line.

It's not enough to look at the mirrors – you must act sensibly on what you see!

Be aware that signals will not always cancel automatically.

51

What You Have To Do To Pass

Always be prepared to slow down or stop. Never assume any one else will give way to you.

As a guideline, ask yourself: "Could I walk across?" If yes, then you could drive across!

If conditions allow and the road is clear – go for it!

Uphill starts may occur on any part of the test . . .

. . . So too might downhill starts.

On angled starts, control the speed with clutch control. Don't let the car swing out too wide.

. . . of course if all else fails you can always rely on your lucky charms . . .

What You Have To Do To Pass

With constant practice you will acquire 'road sense' and become accustomed to being among traffic.

Practice only what you have been taught by your A.D.I.

If your proposed supervisor doesn't qualify, don't risk it! – both you and he could acquire penalty points on your driving licences!

Aim to be at 'test standard' at least four weeks before your test.

Although you will generally have an hour's drive before the test, use it as a warm up, rather than a lesson.

SUMMARY 12
What You Have To Do To Pass

* **Drive consistently safely**

* **Don't endanger other road users**

* **Practice as much as you can**

* **Drive as you do normally. Don't put on a 'show' for the examiner**

* **Passing first time is not a matter of luck**

* **Practice and good tuition are necessary**

* **Take professional advice**

* **Don't be influenced by others into taking a test too early**

About 20% of test candidates pass at their first attempt.

*Be able to drive consistently well **without** assistance from your Instructor.*

Family and friends will be all too pleased to give well meaning advice.

However, your A.D.I. will have the experience and training to best advise you.

Make sure you understand what the test is about and what the examiner will look for.

Take mock tests under strict test conditions, with no talking except for directions.

Hints To Help You Pass First Time

Learn, and understand, the Highway Code thoroughly.

When it is safe and correct to do so keep up with the traffic flow. This shows confidence.

Be ready to proceed when it is safe at junctions.

Aim to be at test standard at least 4 weeks before your test.

Do not take your test early 'for the experience', it will be the examiner who has the experience.

SUMMARY 13
Hints To Help You Pass First Time

* Follow the advice your A.D.I. gives you – it's in your own best interest

* Taking a test too early is a waste of your time and money

* Remember that practice makes perfect

CHAPTER 14

HIGHWAY CODE QUESTIONS ???

Driving Test Questions About The Highway Code And Other Motoring Matters

These questions are taken from actual tests. Please note that these 100 questions are a representative selection; examiners could ask literally anything from the Highway Code or about other motoring matters.

GULP!
WELL, THIS IS IT

YOU MAY STOP THE ENGINE AND RELEASE THE SEAT BELT...

I'D LIKE TO PUT SOME QUESTIONS TO YOU ON THE HIGHWAY CODE AND OTHER MOTORING MATTERS...

Q1. What does the Highway Code state regarding the flashing of headlamps?

Q2. If you were driving at 50 mph, how much space do you need to stop in?

Q3. Which two colours does a traffic light show at the same time?

Q4. If you were turning right from a one-way street what position on the road should you be in?

Q5. What is the hard shoulder on the motorway used for?

Q6. What's the rule about a yellow box junction?

Q7. What do two solid white lines along the road mean?

Q8. How much separation distance would you allow between yourself and the car you are following when you're driving on the open road in good conditions?

Q9. What is the overall stopping distance on a good dry road at 40 mph?

Q10. Can you show me the arm signal for slowing down?

Q11. If you were driving at night and the headlights from an oncoming vehicle were dazzling you, what would you do?

Q12. Can you tell me the maximum speed limit on a motorway for this particular vehicle?

Q13. Can you tell me what the flashing amber light means at a pelican crossing?

Q14. Your car starts to skid. What action would you take to help control it?

Q15. Normally you overtake on the right. Sometimes you can pass on the left. Can you name some of those times?

Q16. Driving along you run into fog. What are the first few things you think about doing?

Q17. What do yellow zig-zag lines mean outside a school?

Q18. On a 3 laned motorway what would you use the right-hand lane for?

Q19. If your car broke down on the motorway what would you do? How would you get help?

Q20. At 30 mph on a dry road what is the overall stopping distance?

Q21. Between what times should you not sound your horn?

Q22. On a road with no parked vehicles, and where conditions allow, where would you position your car in relation to the kerb?

Q23. The acceleration lane on a motorway, where is it?

Q24. If you're driving at night on an unlit road, which of your lights would you use if you are following another car?

Q25. What is the cause of 95% of road traffic accidents?

Q26. When you approach traffic lights, the lights are showing amber. What does this mean?

Q27. When there are double white lines along the road and the line nearest to you is continuous, what does this mean?

Q28. Tell me some of the places where you should not park.

Q29. What is the procedure for joining a motorway?

Q30. If you're turning right out of a narrow street where would you position your vehicle?

Q31. What extra precautions would you take in the daytime if it was misty or foggy?

Q32. If you brake very hard and the car skids in a straight line what would you do?

Q33. In a built-up area where you have street lighting, what would the speed limit be?

Q34. If you were driving along the motorway and you missed the exit you wanted, what would you do?

Q35. At 60 mph in good conditions what is your overall stopping distance?

Q36. On a 3 lane motorway when would you use the centre lane?

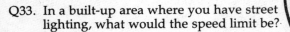

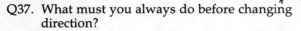

Q37. What must you always do before changing direction?

Q38. Driving down a road with parked vehicles what dangers would you be aware of?

Q39. What should you never leave in an unventilated car when you park?

Q40. What advice does the Highway Code give regarding speed when you're leaving a motorway?

Q41. How does a bus lane work?

Q42. If you're approaching a roundabout and you want to follow the road directly ahead, which is usually the second exit, how would you do that?

Q43. What is the maximum speed limit on a dual carriagway?

Q44. What does the overall stopping distance consist of?

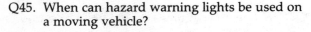

Q45. When can hazard warning lights be used on a moving vehicle?

Q46. In the traffic light sequence, which light follows immediately after the amber light on its own?

Q47. Zig-zag lines at zebra crossings, what do they mean?

Q48. If you were skidding to the left, which way would you steer?

Q49. When would you be allowed to wait in a box junction?

Q50. What's the arm signal for turning left?

Q51. How does drinking alcohol affect driving ability?

Q52. What would you do if the rear of the car skidded to the right?

Q53. Which vehicles are not allowed to use the outside lane of a carriageway with three or more lanes?

Q54. On a right-hand bend what should your position be?

Q55. What precautions should you take when driving in the rain?

Q56. If you're on a country road what special dangers would you be aware of?

Q57. What should you be on the look out for just before you enter your car?

Q58. Travelling at 70 mph what is your overall stopping distance?

Q59. Are you allowed to drive in bus lanes at all?

Q60. What would you do if something fell from your car on the motorway?

Q61. What is the last thing you check before leaving your car?

Q62. How far away from your vehicle should you place a red warning sign?

Q63. Name 5 things you must not do on a motorway.

Q64. If you are first on the scene of an accident, what should you do?

Q65. What do white diagonal stripes in the road mean?

Q66. At an automatic half-barrier level crossing what would you do if the amber lights flash and the alarm starts while you are crossing?

Q67. On a motorway what do flashing amber signals mean?

Q68. What is the 2 second rule?

Q69. How often should you check your tyre pressures?

Q70. When should you give way to a bus?

Q71. What type of signs are triangular?

Q72. You should only use rear fog lights if visibility is reduced to what?

Q73. What fluid levels should you check regularly?

Q74. At a junction in fog what could you do to help locate other traffic?

Q75. What is the one situation when an arm signal should be used?

Q76. How could you tell if a pedestrian is blind and deaf?

Q77. Who should you be particularly aware of at zebra crossings?

HMMM... QUITE HIGH... MIND YOU, IT WAS A VERY STRESSFUL WEEK!

Q78. If a zebra crossing is divided by a central island unit what does this mean?

Q79. How do you turn right off a motorway?

Q80. If you are dazzled by a vehicle behind you, what should you do?

Q81. What is the national speed limit on a single carriageway road?

Q82. What colour, and where, are the studs on the motorway?

Q83. On a 3 lane motorway with no other traffic, what would your position be?

Q84. How should you drive when passing animals?

YO! KEEP YOUR DISTANCE

Q85. On a motorway how would you make other drivers aware of your presence, and why use that particular method?

Q86. What does a parked vehicle in the road tell you?

Q87. When may you remove your seat belt?

Q88. When driving on ice how should you use the controls of the car?

Q89. After driving through a stretch of flooded road what should you do?

Q90. Where may you park at night without lights?

Q91. At a roundabout, which road users should you especially watch out for?

Q92. When turning into a road junction to whom must you give way?

Q93. When driving in lanes what should your position be?

Q94. After overtaking, what must you never do?

Q95. How would you re-join the main carriageway of the motorway from the hard shoulder?

Q96. How would you inform someone controlling traffic that you wanted to go straight ahead?

Highway Code Questions

Q97. When turning right at a junction where there is an oncoming vehicle also turning right, you would generally pass offside-to-offside. Can you tell me when you would pass nearside-to-nearside?

Q98. Before turning left, what must you always check for?

Q99. Which of the traffic light colours means stop?

Q100. When may you cross a solid white line along the road?

CHAPTER 15 HIGHWAY CODE ANSWERS

When giving your answers give them clearly and concisely without going into too much (trivial) detail.

Think about your knowledge as a bottle of milk:

The cream represents the important details – facts about the whole subject (the milk). So don't waffle, just give the examiner the cream; succinct answers to each question.

65

Highway Code Answers

A1. Only use them to make others aware of your presence.

A2. 175ft/53m.

A3. Red and amber.

A4. Well over to the right.

A5. Only for accidents or emergencies.

A6. Do not enter unless your exit is clear.

A7. Do not cross or straddle.

A8. 1 yard/metre for each mph that you are travelling at.

A9. Overall stopping distance is 120ft/36m.

A10. (Wind the window down) Right arm outstretched, palm towards the ground, move your arm slowly up and down.

A11. Slow down or stop.

A12. 70 mph.

A13. Give way to pedestrians on the crossing.

A14. Release the pressure on the footbrake, re- apply the pressure and then pump the brakes if necessary. Steer into the skid.

A15. i) When a vehicle is turning right and you can pass safely on the left.

ii) When you are in the correct lane to turn left at a junction.

iii) When there are queues of slow moving traffic and vehicles in the lane on your right are moving more slowly than you are.

iv) When it is safe to do so in one-way streets.

A16. Slow down, keep a greater distance between yourself and the vehicle you are following. Use dipped headlights. Use windscreen wipers and demisters to keep the screen clean and clear. Don't hang on to the tail lights of the vehicle in front.

A17. Keep entrance clear of stationary vehicles, even if picking up or setting down children.

A18. Overtaking only.

A19. Get it on to the hard shoulder and phone for help from one of the emergency telephones. (Look for symbol on marker posts.)

A20. 75ft/23m.

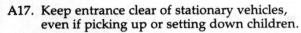

A21. 11.30 p.m. and 7 a.m. (in a built-up area).

A22. 3ft/1m from the nearside kerb.

A23. It is a continuation of the slip road, and is used to build up speed to match that of traffic on the motorway.

A24. Dipped headlights.

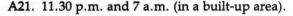

A25. Human error.

A26. Stop, unless you have crossed the white stop line or are so close to it that to pull up would cause an accident.

A27. Do not cross or straddle the solid line nearest to you.

A28. Opposite traffic islands, on or near the brow of a hill, where it would endanger or inconvenience other road users, where it would hide a traffic sign.

A29. Approach on the slip road which will lead into the acceleration lane – use this lane to build up your speed to match that of the traffic on the motorway. Wait for a safe gap and join the inside lane. If there is no safe gap wait at the end of the acceleration lane.

A30. Well to the left.

A31. Use dipped headlights, slow down. Keep a greater distance from the vehicle in front.

A32. Release the pressure on the footbrake, re-apply the pressure and if the car still skids, pump the footbrake.

A33. 30mph.

A34. Continue on the motorway until the next exit.

A35. 240ft/73m.

A36. When there are slower vehicles in the left hand lane.

A37. Check the mirrors.

A38. Vehicle occupants may open doors. Pedestrians (especially children) may walk out between vehicles. Vehicles could drive off without signalling.

A39. Children or animals.

A40. Check the speedometer.

A41. A bus lane operates between certain hours, which will be indicated by a time plate. Outside those hours you may drive in the bus lane.

A42. Approach in the left hand lane, if the roundabout is clear drive around the roundabout in the left hand lane and indicate left at exit before the one you want.

A43. 70mph.

A44. Thinking distance and braking distance.

A45. To warn others briefly if you have to slow down quickly on a motorway or unrestricted (70 m.p.h.) dual-carriageway.

A46. Red.

A47. No overtaking, no stopping, no parking.

A48. To the left.

A49. If you were turning right and are prevented from doing so only by oncoming traffic.

A50. (Wind the window down) Right arm outstretched palm towards the ground, rotate your arm in an anti-clockwise direction.

A51. It reduces co-ordination, increases reaction time and impairs judgement of speed, distance and risk.

A52. Steer to the right.

A53. Goods vehicles of more than 7.5 tonnes Any vehicle pulling a trailer. Buses longer than 40ft/12m.

A54. Well to the left.

A55. Slow down, keep a greater distance from the vehicle in front, use wipers and demisters.

A56. Pedestrians and/or animals in the road, agricultural vehicles.

A57. Cyclists and vehicles.

A58. 315ft/96m.

A59. Yes, outside the bus lane operating times.

A60. Stop at the nearest emergency phone and inform the police. Do not try and retrieve it yourself.

A61. Check over your shoulder before opening the door.

A62. 50 metres. On a motorway 150m.

A63. i) Exceed the speed limit.
ii) Reverse.
iii) Cross the central reservation.
iv) Walk on the carriageway.
v) Stop on the carriageway.

A64. Warn other traffic. Arrange for police/ambulance.

A65. They keep traffic streams apart which may be a danger to each other.
Do not drive over the diagonal stripes (unless to avoid stationary vehicles/obstructions).

A66. Keep going.

A67. Warning of danger: fog, accident or risk of skidding. Keep your speed under 30 mph until you are sure it is safe to go faster.

A68. To ensure you leave a safe gap between your vehicle and the vehicle you are following, use the 2 second rule:- when the vehicle in front passes a fixed point (bridge, telegraph pole) count 2 seconds by saying slowly 1 second, 2 seconds. If you can say this before you reach the fixed point you are following at a safe distance.

_____

A69. Weekly.

A70. When it is signalling to move away, and you can safely give way to it. (In towns.)

A71. Warning signs.

A72. Less than 100m.

A73. Windscreen washer reservoir
Oil
Hydraulic fluid
Radiator
Battery

A74. Open your windows and listen.

A75. When slowing down or stopping for pedestrians to use a zebra crossing.

A76. He would carry a white stick with 2 red reflective bands.

_____

A77. Old people, young children and people with prams.

A78. Treat each half as a separate crossing.

A79. You don't. You must leave by an exit on the left.

A80. Move your head slightly to avoid the dazzle. Do not adjust your mirror as you may not remember to re-set it.

A81. 60 mph.

A82. Red – left hand edge.
Amber – right-hand edge.
Green – marking acceleration and deceleration lanes.
White – separate the lanes.

A83. In the left-hand lane.

A84. Slowly, allow them plenty of room. Do not rev the engine or sound the horn.

A85. Flashing headlamps. The high road noise level may prevent them from hearing your horn.

A86. Road narrows.

A87. When carrying out a manoeuvre that involves reversing.

A88. Very delicately and smoothly.

A89. Dry your brakes, by driving very slowly with your left foot pressing lightly on the brake pedal.

A90. On the road (if in a 30 mph limit) facing direction of traffic flow. In a recognised parking place.

A91. Cyclists.
Motorcyclists.
Long vehicles.

A92. Pedestrians crossing the road into which you are turning.

A93. In the middle of the lane.

A94. Cut in, slow down or stop.

A95. Build up speed on the hard shoulder, joining the inside lane of the motorway when there is a safe gap.

A96. Hold your left hand up to the windscreen, palm facing forwards.

A97. If the layout of the junction or traffic situation makes offside to offside crossing impractical. If indicated by road markings or the position of the other vehicle.

A98. Make sure that a cyclist or motor-cyclist is not coming up from behind on your left.

A99. They all do, except green which means you may go only if the junction is clear.

A100. To enter premises or a side road, to avoid a stationary obstruction, or when ordered to do so by a police officer or traffic warden.

Please note that these 100 questions are only a representative selection; it is important that you study the Highway Code in depth, and put it into practice when you drive.

CHAPTER 16

IDENTIFYING TRAFFIC SIGNS

After the Highway Code questions, the examiner will ask you to identify some traffic signs

IT WAS THE SECOND ON THE LEFT OFFICER

I SHOULD KNOW THIS... AFTER ALL I SPENT THE BEST PART OF 20 MINUTES STUDYING THE HIGHWAY CODE LAST NIGHT...

AS MUCH AS THAT!

. . . If you are not sure of the answer, have an educated guess. If you know the different shapes of signs you will at least be able to say if it is a warning sign, or a sign giving an order, etc.

Identifying Traffic Signs

1

A No small cars
B No double parking
C No overtaking

2

A No black cars
B No large cars
C No vehicles
(except solo motor-cycles scooters or mopeds)

3

A Pick pockets
B Wandering wrinklies
C Elderly people

4

A Ankle biters
B No children
C Children going to and from school

5

A Aliens
B No pedestrians
C Pedestrians in road ahead

6

A Fog
B No nothing
C No vehicles

7

A National speed limit
B No waiting
C No entry

8

A No left turn
B No right turn
C No turning

9

A No left turn
B No right turn
C No U turn

10

A Spokeless zone
B Cycle route ahead
C No cycling

11

A No one over 30
B Maximum speed
C Minimum speed

12

A No rag and bone men
B No horse drawn vehicles
C No deliveries

13

A Bottle bank
B No through road
C Road narrows on both sides

14

A Bridge
B Tunnel
C Black-hole

15

A Moose
B Reindeer
C Wild animals

16

A No pedestrians
B No training shoes
C No footpath

17

A Exploding cars
B Parachutists
C No vehicles carrying explosives

18

A Road narrows
B End of dual-carriageway
C Dead end

19

A Car wash
B Car dump
C Quayside or river bank

20

A Tunnel
B Hump back bridge
C Fly-over

Identifying Traffic Signs

21

A No entry
B 60 mph limit
C National speed limit applies

22

A Give way
B Traffic lights
C Manually operated road works sign

23

A No stopping (clearway)
B No speeding
C No road markings

24

A No grey lorries
B No goods vehicles
C End of goods vehicles restriction

25

A No roof racks
B No overtaking
C No motor vehicles

26

A School crossing patrol
B No children allowed
C Dangerous children

27

A Church
B Crossroads
C T-junction

28

A No lorries with writing on
B No goods vehicles over weight shown
C No vehicles over length shown

29

A What goes up must come down
B Priority over on-coming traffic
C Give priority to vehicles from opposite direction

30

A No vehicles or combination of vehicles over length shown
B No black lorries
C No goods vehicles

31

A Large pins on the road
B Puncture zone
C Loose chippings

32

A Toilets
B Parking
C Passing place

33

A Lane closed ahead
B Stop
C No entry

34

A No mountain bikes
B No cycling
C Cycle route

35

A One way
B Mini roundabout
C Contra flow

36

Hemel Hempstead 7 B 486

A Dead end
B Motorway sign
C Local direction sign

37

A Temporary maximum speed
B Temperature (farenheit)
C Maximum number of cars

38

A Roundabout
B Ring road
C Reduce speed

39

A No mobile phones
B No outgoing calls
C Direction of nearest telephone

40

A Route for cycles only
B No cycling
C Cyclists dismount

41
A Uneven road surface
B Double humpback bridge
C Beware of camels

42
A One way
B Ahead only
C No way

43
A Traffic merging from left
B Sharp bend
C Dual carriageway

44
A Airport
B Delays ahead
C Low flying aircraft

45
A No personalised number plates
B No vehicles over weight shown
C No entry on the 20th of each month

46
A Turn right only
B One way
C Exit

47
A No vehicles over width shown
B No fat people
C Tunnel

48
A Turn right only
B Ahead only
C Turn left only

49
A Steep hill
B No giraffes
C No vehicles over height shown

50
A Red Indians
B Railway
C Two way traffic ahead

1.	C	28.	B
2.	C	29.	C
3.	C	30.	A
4.	C	31.	C
5.	C	32.	B
6.	C	33.	A
7.	C	34.	B
8.	A	35.	B
9.	B	36.	C
10.	B	37.	A
11.	B	38.	B
12.	B	39.	C
13.	C	40.	A
14.	B	41.	A
15.	C	42.	B
16.	A	43.	A
17.	C	44.	C
18.	B	45.	B
19.	C	46.	A
20.	B	47.	A
21.	C	48.	C
22.	C	49.	C
23.	A	50.	C
24.	C		
25.	C		
26.	A		
27.	B		

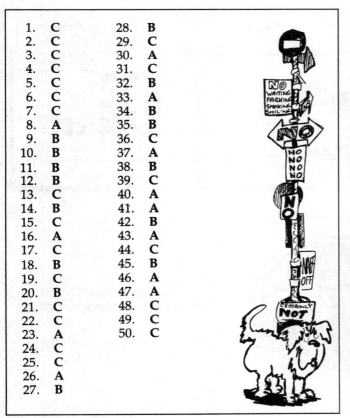

. . . Give your answers clearly; don't waffle or give unnecessary detail.

Even if you don't know the precise meaning of a sign, if you know what the shape signifies you should be able to work out what the sign is telling you.

CIRCLES GIVE ORDERS

Red rings or Circles give a negative instruction

Vehicles with over 12 seats

Blue circles give a positive instruction

must keep left.

RECTANGLES INFORM

You have priority over vehicles from opposite direction.

. . . there are exceptions

TRIANGLES WARN

STOP

Even if the writing is obscured by snow, the shape (octagonal) will tell you what it means.

Because this is such an important sign, the shape is only used for this.

CHAPTER 17 WHEN YOU PASS

* Initially, just drive on routes you know

* Drive in quiet periods

* Make sure you're familiar with the car

* Don't drink

So, you've passed your test and can finally drive on your own . . .

Free to go where you like, when you like . . .

You may have to pass a family test first though!

At first you may feel self-conscious as a 'new'-driver.

Don't worry, just relax and drive as you have been taught.

You can now decide where to go, so plan your route before hand.

When You Pass

Initially drive in daylight during quiet times to get used to the car.

Find out what it runs on and where the filler cap is.

You might think that the family car is not your style.

Ideally you'd prefer a car more suited to your character . . .

Maybe a sports saloon, with C.D. player and graphic equalizer.

Reality intrudes however, when you check-up on the insurance.

Start off with a lower powered more affordable car.

The insurance will be a lot less, as will general running costs.

Having acquired a car, you'll want to use it at every opportunity.

And of course you'll want to keep it looking immaculate.

Don't overload your car – this could dangerously affect braking and steering.

It is advisable to have a motorway lesson with your A.D.I.

Having passed your test there are ways in which your driving can be improved.

Some Police Driving Schools run civilian courses which include skid-pan training.

If you want to learn to race or rally there are courses available.

Advanced road driving tests can be taken to improve your driving.

Your A.D.I. should be able to advise you on advanced driving and tests.

SUMMARY 17
When You Pass

* **Take it easy at first**
* **Familiarise yourself with the car you will drive**
* **Have motorway driving lessons**
* **Consider taking Advanced Driving Tests – this may reduce your insurance**

CHAPTER 18 — BEING A GREEN MOTORIST
by Annette Dudek

Recent figures show that in one year vehicle emissions produced:
* 4½ million tonnes of carbon monoxide
* Over 1 million tonnes of nitrogen oxides
* Over ½ million tonnes of hydrocarbons

The phrase 'green motorist' is a contradiction in terms.

CARS CAUSE POLLUTION: AIR

EXHAUST GASES CONTRIBUTE TO ACID RAIN, THE GREENHOUSE EFFECT, GLOBAL WARMING, SMOG, AND MAY CAUSE CANCER

The health of 1 in 5 of the population is at increased risk from air pollution.

CARS CAUSE POLLUTION: LAND

Presently most old cars are dumped, causing eyesores on the land and environmental problems.

CARS CAUSE POLLUTION: WATER

I'LL PUT THE WASTE OIL DOWN THE DRAIN — A FEW PINTS WON'T DO ANY HARM

Water pollution occurs when oil is washed off roads or illegally dumped down drains.

CARS USE UP: FUEL RESOURCES

OIL R US

Motor vehicles consume one third of the world's supply of oil (a finite resource).

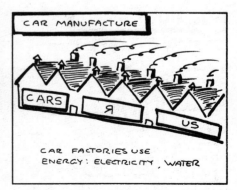

CAR MANUFACTURE

CARS R US

CAR FACTORIES USE ENERGY: ELECTRICITY, WATER

The process of making new cars is energy intensive and polluting in itself.

Being A Green Motorist

* People are not very willing to give up the freedom and convenience of a private car

* There are, however, steps that everybody can take to minimise the environmental impact

* First 'green' your car!

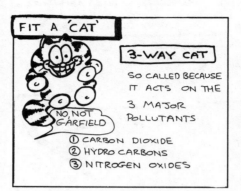

Using a 3-way catalytic converter harmful emissions could be reduced by 90%.

Unleaded fuel is cheaper and less harmful to the environment.

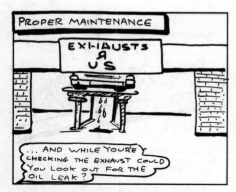

Look after your car by keeping it well maintained, check for holes in the exhaust and oil leaks.

Go for durability and aim to keep your car for as long as possible.

Smaller cars produce less pollution by burning less fuel and taking less energy to build.

If everybody did as much as they could individually it would contribute to a healthier environment.

Drive with vehicle sympathy – no harsh acceleration or braking.

Most carbon dioxide is emitted during the first few miles of a journey.

Walk, cycle, or take the bus.

Where possible, car sharing is an ideal way of reducing the amount of vehicles on the road.

Worldwide there are 400 million motor vehicles – what are other countries doing?

WHAT IN THE WORLD'S GOING ON?

SWEDEN
* An experiment is being carried out whereby every car entering Stockholm's inner limits has to pay a monthly fee of 300 Kroner (about £30)
* Ultimately, computers will monitor vehicle entry and exit

NETHERLANDS
* Has a long history of promoting cycling, walking and public transport
* Financial incentives to buy 'cat' cars
* Plans to reduce motor travel by 40% by 2015
* In 1990 tram, train and bus travel were made free to young people

BRITAIN
* By 1993, catalytic converters must be fitted to new cars
* November 1991 – exhaust emission requirement for M.O.T. Test
* As from April 1991 all new cars must be able to run on unleaded petrol (introduced 1986)
* Various cities and towns are operating 'traffic calming' schemes
* These include 20 mph limits, chicanes, and raised areas (humps)
* These measures are all designed to reduce speed in residential areas

GERMANY
* Introduced unleaded petrol in 1984
* All taxis run on diesel engines
* Tax incentives for 'greener' motoring in 1985
* Regulation of catalytic converters in 1988
* Cities have much restricted parking and traffic calming areas
* BMW is building a re-cycling plant
* Mercedes avoid using plastics
* Volkswagen (with a government grant) has set up a recycling project, using unemployed people

FRANCE
* Encourages use of small cars by tax incentives
* Anybody can ride a moped
* Car advertising is strictly regulated
* Fastest rail network (TGVF) in the world

GREECE
* 1988 a scheme was introduced whereby cars with registration numbers ending in an odd number could enter the city centre only on alternate days. On other days cars ending with even numbers could enter
* In theory it sounded fine. However, people bought an additional car to enable them to enter the city each day.
* Generally this second car was an old banger adding even more pollution
* End of scheme – back to the drawing board

SWITZERLAND
* Zurich is the best example of a city coping well with transport problems
* Trams have priority over other traffic and provide highly efficient and reliable public transport

FISA
* FISA (motorsport's governing body) has created a new commission to draw up technical rules for battery and solar powered cars
* Electric cars could be racing in Britain in 1993

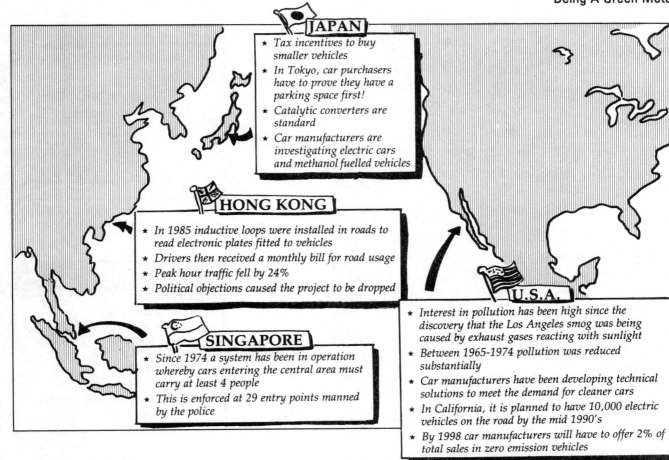

JAPAN

★ Tax incentives to buy smaller vehicles
★ In Tokyo, car purchasers have to prove they have a parking space first!
★ Catalytic converters are standard
★ Car manufacturers are investigating electric cars and methanol fuelled vehicles

HONG KONG

★ In 1985 inductive loops were installed in roads to read electronic plates fitted to vehicles
★ Drivers then received a monthly bill for road usage
★ Peak hour traffic fell by 24%
★ Political objections caused the project to be dropped

SINGAPORE

★ Since 1974 a system has been in operation whereby cars entering the central area must carry at least 4 people
★ This is enforced at 29 entry points manned by the police

U.S.A.

★ Interest in pollution has been high since the discovery that the Los Angeles smog was being caused by exhaust gases reacting with sunlight
★ Between 1965-1974 pollution was reduced substantially
★ Car manufacturers have been developing technical solutions to meet the demand for cleaner cars
★ In California, it is planned to have 10,000 electric vehicles on the road by the mid 1990's
★ By 1998 car manufacturers will have to offer 2% of total sales in zero emission vehicles

Being A Green Motorist

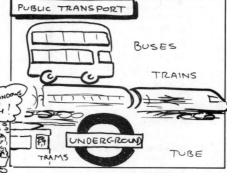

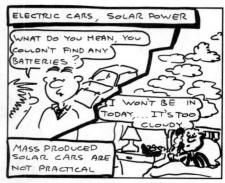

The more roads there are, the more cars there are to fill them!

A good public transport system could substantially reduce the number of vehicles on the roads.

Electric cars are 'clean' themselves, but producing electricity can cause pollution.

The argument against diesel cars is that some of the emissions are thought to cause cancer.

Until the world's governments come up with stricter legislation on the use of roads and cars . . .

. . . It must remain with the conscience of the individual motorist.

CHAPTER 19 CANDIDATES QUESTIONS

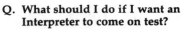

PLEASE CAN I GO TO THE TOILET

Q. What are the times of the tests?
A. 0840
   0930
   1030
   1120
   1210
   1355
   1445
   1535

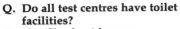

Q. Do all test centres have toilet facilities?
A. No. Check with your Instructor: He will know the local area and can advise you. (Some test centres do have toilets; either separately male and female, or one shared facility.)

Q. What should I do if I want an Interpreter to come on test?
A. After you sign your name, say to the examiner 'I'd like my Interpreter to accompany me', or get him to say it!

Q. How long does the test last?
A. From leaving the waiting room to the examiner leaving the car, about 40 minutes. The actual drive may last approximately 25-35 minutes depending on traffic conditions.

Q. Are test centres 'no-smoking'?
A. Yes. If you want to smoke, have one outside the test centre before you go in.

Q. Do all test centres have car parks?
A. No. Some purpose built centres do have car parks. Otherwise it is on-street parking, (this may be reserved for test candidates). Avoid parking more than 10 minutes before your test; you might get in the way of previous candidates.

Candidate's Questions

Q. If I want my Instructor to come on test with me, what do I do?

A. After signing your name, say to the examiner: "I'd like my Instructor to accompany me on test". Examiners generally welcome this and would not object. It must be you that asks, this is because it is your test. If he accompanies you, your Instructor must take no part in the test.

Q. Do I need to take a pen to sign with?

A. No, the examiner will provide one.

Q. If for some reason I haven't got proof of identity can I still take the test?

A. No. Quite categorically you must be able to provide acceptable proof of identity:
Driving licence
Passport
Employer's Identity Card
or other proof showing your photograph and your signature.
If your licence is unsigned and no other proof can be provided the test will not take place.

Q. If I take the test in a private car will I need to show the M.O.T. and Insurance Certificate?

A. No. It is your responsibility to ensure that the car you provide is suitably insured and roadworthy.

Q. Do they have a special machine to do the eye sight test?

A. No. The examiner will ask you to read the registration number of a vehicle which he identifies.

Q. What happens if I forget my glasses on the day of the test?

A. If you cannot read the number plate at the required distance, you will fail the test.

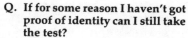

Q. **I've failed a test. How long do I have to wait before I can take another?**

A. One calendar month. This is to enable you to rectify any fault(s) that caused you to fail.

Q. **Can I take my test in a van?**

A. Yes, provided that the examiner is able to see clearly through the rear window.
Also it must not be loaded or partly loaded, must not be over 7.5 tonnes and must have a forward facing front passenger seat.
NOTE: In a van you would not be asked to demonstrate the reverse parking exercise.
Also note that you will be asked to reverse into a limited opening on the *right*.

Q. **I've got a large American car which is left hand drive. Can I take my test in it?**

A. Yes. Obviously though you would need to take extra care and be particularly diligent in your use of mirrors.

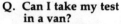

Q. **If I want to postpone my test, how much notice do I have to give without losing the fee?**

A. 10 clear working days; not counting the day on which the Traffic Area Office received your notification, the day of the appointment, Saturdays, Sundays, Bank Holidays, Christmas Day and Good Friday.

Q. **What happens if I'm late for my test appointment?**

A. The test will not proceed. Test programmes are planned within strict timetables. If one candidate is late this will obviously have a domino effect on all other tests.

Q. **I'm just about to take another driving test. Will I get the same examiner and will he remember me?**

A. Candidates are allocated to examiners on a purely random basis, so, yes you could have the same examiner. He may remember you, but with 8 tests a day, 40 tests per week etc, they see a lot of people so it is unlikely that he will have instant recall of your last test.

Candidate's Questions

DON'T WORRY ABOUT GEORGE IN THE BACK

Q. I've heard that sometimes the examiner has someone with him. Is this true?

A. Yes. Examiner's work is checked by supervising examiners. They 'sit in' on tests to observe the examiner at work. If this happens on your test, don't worry about it! The supervising examiner will not take any part in the test, but will sit quietly in the back. Consider the extra weight though, and discuss with your A.D.I. the effect that this will have on braking etc.

Q. Can I drive alone as soon as I've passed my test?

A. As long as you're covered by insurance, yes. It is a good idea to photocopy all relevant documents before sending them off.

Q. If I'm driving on an International Driving Licence, do I have to put 'L' plates on the car for a test?

A. No. 'L' plates are required only for provisional licence holders. However, as an International Licence holder if you do not pass the UK test within 12 months of your arrival in this country you will be restricted as a Provisional Licence holder.

COMPASS

FLARES

BETTER PACK THESE JUST IN CASE I GET LOST.

Q. I'm thinking about taking an intensive week's course with a test. Is this a good idea?

A. It very much depends on you as an individual and how best you learn. Think carefully about the amount of learning involved (possibly 5 hours per day) and your own personal limits.

Q. I don't know the area that I'm taking my test in. Is that a problem?

A. No. The examiners will direct you, so it is not necessary to know the town or area. However, driving around the area (keep off test routes – your A.D.I. will know these) may help you to familiarise yourself with the local hazards etc.

Q. I get very nervous before tests. Should I take some tablets to help me with this?

A. Try to get to the root cause of your nervousness; discuss this with your A.D.I. Perhaps mock tests will help you to overcome it. Only as a very last resort should you consider taking anything, and then only after consulting with your doctor.

94

If there is Fog, Ice, Snow or High winds on the day of your test . . .

Contact the test centre on the phone number shown on your appointment card, and ask their advice. If you are on an 0840 am test (first of the day) ask your A.D.I.'s advice.

If traffic lights are not working, you should . . .

Be extremely careful: no-one has priority, so use your best judgement in deciding whether to wait or go on.

If pelican lights are not working, you should . . .

Treat it as a zebra crossing. However, be aware that pedestrians and other motorists may be unaware of this and may be confused.

What If . . . ? Coping With All Eventualities

You come across a vehicle unloading goods. There are continuous white lines along the road . . .

In these circumstances it is allowable for you to cross the solid lines. Obviously though, make sure it is safe to do so.

You want to turn right, but there is already a vehicle waiting in the safety zone. What do you do?

Wait in the diagonal stripes behind the vehicle already waiting to turn right in these circumstances. This is the safest place to wait.

If anything unusual or unexpected happens on test, demonstrate to the examiner that you can cope in a safe and common sense way.

Expect the unexpected and you'll never be caught unawares!

CHAPTER 21
How To Avoid Accidents

... HOW MANY

On average, each year there are at least 5,000 deaths through road accidents. This is equivalent to 14 full Jumbo Jets.

COUNTING THE NUMBERS

NOT VERY ENVIRONMENTALLY FRIENDLY, ARE WE SIR?

Details are collected for all accidents where injury or death occurred. Damage only accidents are not recorded.

ANALYSING THE INFORMATION

BOFFIN-O-METER

These figures enable causes to be pin pointed. Types of accident etc. can be detected.

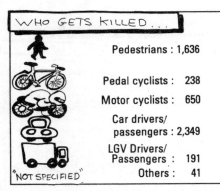

WHO GETS KILLED ...

Pedestrians :	1,636
Pedal cyclists :	238
Motor cyclists :	650
Car drivers/ passengers :	2,349
LGV Drivers/ Passengers :	191
Others :	41

"NOT SPECIFIED"

These figures are for 1990, the latest available.
Source: RAGB 1990 HMSO

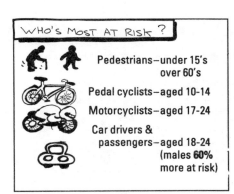

WHO'S MOST AT RISK?

Pedestrians – under 15's over 60's

Pedal cyclists – aged 10-14

Motorcyclists – aged 17-24

Car drivers & passengers – aged 18-24 (males 60% more at risk)

So why are the particular groups above most at risk?

PEDESTRIANS

I'M 83 YOU KNOW

Youngsters are not as aware of danger as adults. Elderly people may have impaired vision or hearing and be slower to move.

How To Avoid Accidents

Again, this age group does not have the perception of danger that adults do.

Motorcyclists are particularly vulnerable with little protection from other vehicles and elements.

Lack of experience and an attitude of 'it couldn't happen to me' are major causes of accidents in this group.

*95% of all accidents are caused by human error : the driver : **you**.*

Roads and cars do not have accidents – it's the human element that causes them.

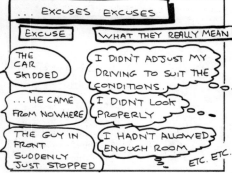

Drivers involved in accidents will usually blame everything except themselves.

A major factor in road accidents is the attitude and behaviour of drivers.

As an 'L' driver your only reason to be in the car was to drive.

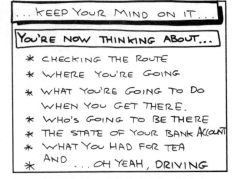

However, when qualified, driving becomes (wrongly) secondary to the reason you are in the car.

Most accidents happen within a few miles of home, or on routes that are very familiar.

If your view is restricted, assume that someone is there. One day there will be!

Never assume, or think, that others will do the correct thing!

How To Avoid Accidents

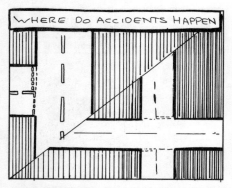

Most accidents happen within a 20 m area of junctions.

Twice as many accidents happen leaving a main road, as entering a main road.

Junctions present the biggest hazard because road users join, meet and cross; situations involving potential conflict.

Road signs and markings should be noted, and acted upon.

Again, do not assume that a driver will react in a certain way; make sure!

Overtaking is one of the most dangerous manoeuvres that a driver can carry out. Sometimes it is the last manoeuvre a driver carries out.

Statistics show that the winter months October, November and December have high accident rates!

This is due to weather conditions and dark mornings and evenings.

Fridays have the highest accident figures — due to more people being about.

Accident rates peak between 10 pm and midnight for young males aged 17 to 20.

However this peak rapidly declines after the age of 28.

Although accidents happen more frequently at certain times, they can literally happen at anytime.

How To Avoid Accidents

The figures above are for a driving career spanning 17-70 years of age.

Don't put yourself in situations where your safety is compromised!

Driving safely means being consistent – it only takes one fatal error!

Each time you reduce your safety margins, you increase the risk.

Never assume you have right of way – other people may think the same thing.

A moments loss of temper could have far reaching consequences.

UNDER THE INFLUENCE

Alcohol affects your driving ability:

* You take longer to react
* Reduces your concentration
* Gives a false sense of confidence
* You are less able to judge speed and distance

About 30% of all people killed in road accidents were 'over the limit'.

If you are planning to drive, do not drink anything alcoholic.

If you are going out in a group elect a 'dry' driver, or get a taxi.

Medicines can make you feel drowsy or unco-ordinated – consult your doctor.

Both illness and tiredness will slow your reactions and dull your senses.

Having an accident could be most inconvenient – you could end up dead.

THEN + NOW

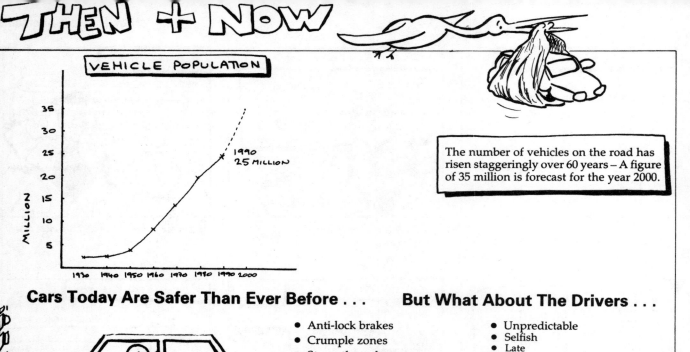

VEHICLE POPULATION

The number of vehicles on the road has risen staggeringly over 60 years – A figure of 35 million is forecast for the year 2000.

1990
25 MILLION

Cars Today Are Safer Than Ever Before . . .

- Anti-lock brakes
- Crumple zones
- Strengthened areas
- Cruise control
- Front & rear seat belts
- Air bag

But What About The Drivers . . .

- Unpredictable
- Selfish
- Late
- . . . got a headache
- On the phone
- It was the other guy's fault . . .
- Sorry mate, I didn't see you
- 'Course I checked my mirror
- But I do own the road
- I'm a man aren't I?

How To Avoid Accidents

Driving is 90% seeing, and 10% doing.

Unfortunately most drivers look but don't see.

Consider all possibilities: one day it **will** happen.

Driver's actions or movements can often give clues as to their intentions.

Before acting on others signals, make sure it is safe.

SUMMARY 21
How To Avoid Accidents

* Plan ahead
* Expect the unexpected
* Don't put yourself or others at risk
* Concentrate fully whilst driving
* Never assume you have right of way

Research Has Shown That Certain Types Of Drivers Have A Much Lower Accident Rate:

High Mileage Drivers
(over 30,000 miles per year)

Because they are in traffic situations so frequently, they learn from experience that given a particular set of circumstances there will probably be a predicted outcome.

This experience shows itself as a 'feeling' or intuition that something will happen; ie, a car will change lanes suddenly and without apparent warning, maybe the experienced motorist has noticed arm movements as the steering wheel is about to be turned, or a slight movement of the driver's head.

Quite often experienced drivers react to situations almost subconsciously; their mind has processed all available information (through eyes, ears etc) and has compared it with previous circumstances to plan a course of action – sometimes before they even consciously think about it.

OH NO...
NOT THIS
AGAIN...

Advanced Drivers

This group are generally more interested in driving than the average motorist, and they have a higher awareness of road safety and the causes of accidents.

Having taken an advanced test indicates that they can drive to a system (for dealing with hazards) which ultimately must be safer than a haphazard approach.

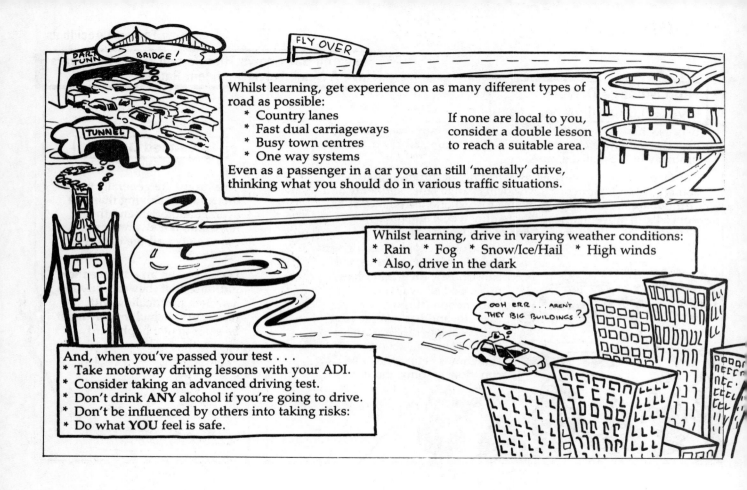

Whilst learning, get experience on as many different types of road as possible:
* Country lanes
* Fast dual carriageways
* Busy town centres
* One way systems

If none are local to you, consider a double lesson to reach a suitable area.

Even as a passenger in a car you can still 'mentally' drive, thinking what you should do in various traffic situations.

Whilst learning, drive in varying weather conditions:
* Rain   * Fog   * Snow/Ice/Hail   * High winds
* Also, drive in the dark

And, when you've passed your test . . .
* Take motorway driving lessons with your ADI.
* Consider taking an advanced driving test.
* Don't drink **ANY** alcohol if you're going to drive.
* Don't be influenced by others into taking risks:
* Do what **YOU** feel is safe.

At the time, your driving test can seem like an enormous hurdle; deliberately designed to thwart you.

However, don't forget the aim of the driving test: TO REDUCE ROAD ACCIDENTS.

You will help to do this by always driving with:

Care
Consideration
Courtesy

CHAPTER 23 THE FUTURE OF THE TEST

POSSIBLE CHANGES

* **Written tests**

* **Professional supervision**

* **Motorway training**

* **Probationary plates**

MULTIPLE CHOICE...

A TEST PAPER OF 100 QUESTIONS COULD COVER MANY ASPECTS OF MOTORING.

RIGHT, YOU HAVE ONE HOUR

A written test would be taken before a practical driving test could be taken.

MOTORWAY SANITY

BEFORE A TEST CERTIFICATE COULD BE EXCHANGED FOR A FULL LICENCE, A COURSE OF MOTORWAY TUITION WOULD NEED TO BE TAKEN

A course of 5 hours motorway training could be a life-saver!

ONLY QUALIFIED SUPERVISION

UNQUALIFIED TUITION COULD CAUSE CONFUSION AND A CONFLICT OF LEARNING...

OK SON, THESE ARE THE TRAFFICATORS OF THE MOTOR VEHICLE, BLAH, BLAH BLAH...

WHAT??

Taking tuition from an Approved Driving Instructor would ensure learners are taught only correct and safe techniques.

P PLATES...

CAN I HAVE A P PLEASE, BOB?

OH NO, IT'S A P PLATE DRIVER

AAAGH

Probationary plates could warn other motorists of new drivers!

SUMMARY 23
Future Changes

* A written theory test would ensure a certain minimum knowledge of motoring laws etc, before a driver is allowed on the road

* Motorway tuition would ensure at least that new drivers were aware of correct procedure

Q1. Why was the driving test introduced?
- a) To create jobs ☐
- b) To reduce road accidents ☐
- c) To make life dificult ☐

VROOM VROOM

Q2. How much did the driving test initially cost?
- a) £21.50 ☐
- b) 7/6d ☐
- c) 37½p ☐

Q3. Why are pelican crossings so called?
- a) Lord Pelican invented them ☐
- b) The first one was by the pelican house at London Zoo ☐
- c) The letters stand for PEdestrian LIght CONtrolled crossing ☐

Q4. When was the driving test introduced?
- a) 1935 ☐
- b) 1947 ☐
- c) 1963 ☐

Q5. When were zebra crossings first introduced?
- a) 1935 ☐
- b) 1951 ☐
- c) 1971 ☐

Q6. When was the reverse parking exercise introduced into the driving test?
- a) 1st April 1991 ☐
- b) 1st May 1935 ☐
- c) 1st June 1975 ☐

Q7. What is the first part of the ADI (Approved Driving Instructors) exam?
a) Instructional ability ☐
b) Driving test ☐
c) Written test ☐

Q8. ADIs have to pass how many tests?
a) None ☐
b) 4 ☐
c) 3 ☐

Q9. What colour is the ADI certificate of registration?
a) Red ☐
b) Orange ☐
c) Green ☐

Q10. Any person giving driving tuition for payment must be:
a) Over 35 ☐
b) A good driver ☐
c) Department of Transport approved ☐

Q11. What is the 3rd test that ADIs must pass?
a) Patience ☐
b) Diplomacy ☐
c) Instructional ability ☐

Q12. What are the criteria regarding accompanying a learner driver?
a) Must have a full licence ☐
b) Must be over 25 ☐
c) Must be 21 at least and have held a full British licence for at least 3 years ☐

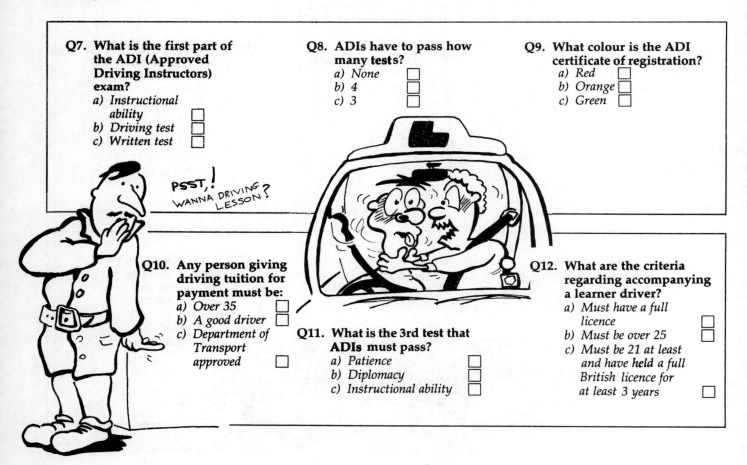

PSST,! WANNA DRIVING LESSON?

Q13. **When should you apply for your test?**
a) As soon as possible ☐
b) When your ADI advises you ☐
c) When you feel like it ☐

Q14. **How will you be advised of your test appointment?**
a) By phone ☐
b) By fax ☐
c) By post ☐

Q15. **If you want to change the date of your test (without losing your fee) how much notice must you give?**
a) 24 hours ☐
b) 7 days ☐
c) 10 days ☐

Q16. **How many applications can you make at any one time?**
a) 6 ☐
b) 199 ☐
c) one ☐

Q17. **When you receive your appointment card who should you advise?**
a) No one ☐
b) Your ADI ☐
c) The local police ☐

Q18. **Approximately how many tests are conducted each year?**
a) 24 million ☐
b) 4 million ☐
c) 2 million ☐

Motoring Quiz

Q19. Which age group is most successful in the test?
 a) 21-40 ☐
 b) Under 21 ☐
 c) 41-50 ☐

Q20. Which gender has the higher pass rate?
 a) Male ☐
 b) Female ☐

Q21. Where do examiners come from?
 a) Mars ☐
 b) A factory in Walsall ☐
 c) All walks of life ☐

Q22. Which region has the highest pass rate?
 a) Scottish ☐
 b) Metropolitan ☐
 c) S. Wales ☐

Q23. You should contact the Traffic Area Office if you haven't received your test appointment within:
 a) 4 weeks ☐
 b) 3 weeks ☐
 c) 2 weeks ☐

Q24. What is the first stage for would-be examiners?
 a) Instructing ☐
 b) Interview ☐
 c) Driving test ☐

Q25. Can ADIs examine as well?
a) Yes ☐
b) Sometimes ☐
c) No ☐

Q26. How many minor faults will fail you on test?
a) 7 ☐
b) 12 ☐
c) Minor faults alone will not fail you ☐

Q27. Can you fail on the Highway Code alone?
a) No ☐
b) Yes ☐
c) Sometimes ☐

Q28. How much training do examiners have initially?
a) 6 weeks ☐
b) 4 weeks ☐
c) None ☐

Q29. How long does the driving test last?
a) 15 minutes ☐
b) 25-30 minutes ☐
c) Too long ☐

Q30. What is the eyesight distance requirement for the 'L' test?
a) 67ft / 20.5m ☐
b) 90ft / 27.5m ☐
c) 75.3 car lengths ☐

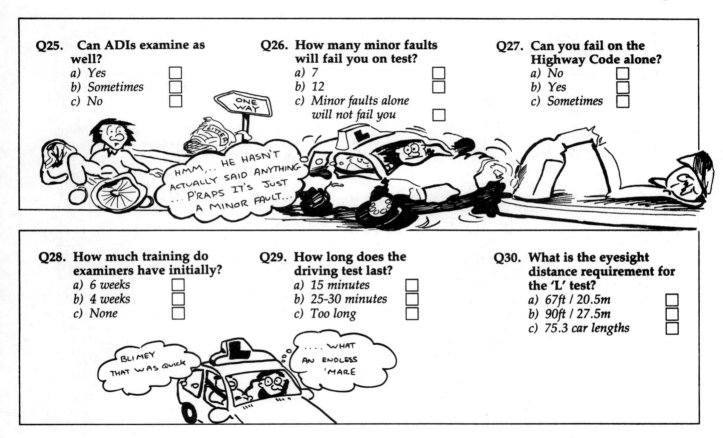

1.	B	22.	A
2.	B	23.	B
3.	C	24.	C
4.	A	25.	C
5.	B	26.	C
6.	A	27.	B
7.	C	28.	B
8.	C	29.	B
9.	C	30.	A
10.	C		
11.	C		
12.	C		
13.	B		
14.	C		
15.	C		
16.	C		
17.	B		
18.	C		
19.	B		
20.	A		
21.	C		

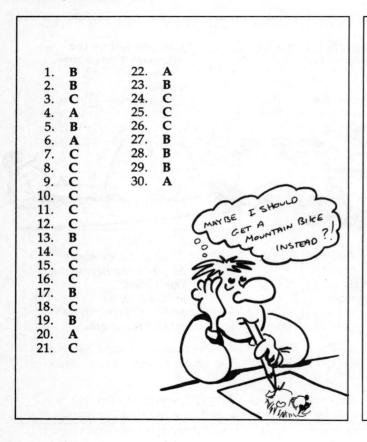

How Did You Score?

0-9: What a sad uncharismatic person you are. Driving test? Forget it. Stick to breeding yoghurts or knitting stamps.

10-19: Have you read this book or what? More study is definitely needed if you are going to stand any chance of passing your test.

20-24: Most average. Very middle of the road. OK. Almost agreeable. So-so . . . quite.

25-30: SAFE! If you haven't cheated this is a good score. If your practical driving ability matches your theoretical knowledge you should have no problems passing your test.

over 30: Maths was never your strong point was it?

CHAPTER 25   POST SCRIPT: A PERSONAL VIEW   By Vicki Stone

For my 17 year old daughter Kate and her teenage friends, the next challenge after passing their 'O' levels was the driving test.

They started off the right way; professional instruction, and supervision by their parents.

One evening, shortly after passing her driving test, one of the girls was persuaded to act as a 'supervisor' to a friend who was learning to drive.

My daughter Kate and another friend were passengers that night. Despite atrocious weather conditions the driver went far too fast. Although the girl was 'supervising' him she herself had limited driving experience, and, as the car was not fitted with dual-controls, could not physically intervene. She pleaded with the driver to slow down, but to no avail. Attempting to overtake, in heavy rain, the car went out of control. In the resulting crash two of the four occupants were killed.

One of them was my daughter Kate.

The judge said that the driver "was showing off in front of friends" and sentenced him to 9 months youth custody. Three families would never be the same again.

As Kate's mother, I felt that this accident should never have been allowed to happen. I soon discovered that in most other countries it would not have happened because inexperienced drivers are prevented from supervising learners. I was determined that Kate's death should not be in vain, and I began a campaign to change the law. The **Learn and Live** campaign was started to prevent inexperienced drivers from supervising learners. With tremendous public support I persuaded the powers-that-be to close this loop hole in the law. On the 12th July 1990, the second anniversary of Kate's death, the Minister of Transport announced that supervisors of learner drivers would have to be at least 21 years of age, and have held a full British driving licence for at least 3 years.

Having achieved this objective, the **Learn and Live** campaign is now asking the Government for a probationary period between the test and a full driving licence. This would enable new drivers to gain valuable experience whilst at the same time minimising danger to both themselves and others.

Research has shown that 1 in 3 young male drivers have an accident within 2 years of passing the driving test. During the initial campaign I had received many letters from parents whose sons and daughters had become part of the statistics. Another contributory factor is that teenage drivers admit that their driving is worse when their friends are passengers.

During the proposed probationary period I would like to see the following restrictions apply:

1. **Compulsory display** of 'P' (probationary) or 'R' (restricted) plates.

2. **Limitation of passengers,** carriage of only one young passenger unless accompanied by a mature adult (over 21).

3. **Compulsory motorway tuition** before being allowed to drive on them unaccompanied.

4. **Length of probationary period** to be set at two years; only waived on passing a recognised advanced driving test.

5. **Insurance group limitation,** to groups 1, 2 and 3, unless accompanied by a mature passenger over 21.

6. **No towing** of caravans or trailers.

7. **Zero alcohol** level whilst learning and during probationary period.

8. **A further probationary period** would follow any serious driving offence.

The Driving Standards Agency (D.S.A.) strongly recommends that learner drivers study the 'Syllabus for learning to drive a car'. Within that syllabus it is stated that learner drivers should know "which road users are most at risk", and should also "be aware of age dependent problems among other road users especially among children, teenagers and the elderly".

These vulnerable road users can be clearly identified. New drivers, also vulnerable, cannot be distinguished from any other motorist! A plate indicating a novice driver would protect both themselves and others.

If you feel you would like to support the **Learn and Live** campaign, please write to: **Vicki Stone**
P.O. Box 7
Kingswinford
West Midlands
DY6 9QZ